WHEN GOD
CALLS

Will you trust Me now?

GLENN PEMBERTON

Cover design by M.E. Hall

ISBN: 978-0-89098-366-9

Dedication

To David, T'auna

and Pam

Acknowledgements

This book began in 2004 as a series of workshops at Oklahoma Christian University for local preachers, organized by Shon Smith, then Vice President for Church Relations at the university. Shon not only invited my participation, but also suggested the topic, encouraged publication, read early drafts of the manuscript, and offered numerous helpful suggestions. I want to thank Shon and the original seminar participants for their enthusiastic response to the material and their help along the way.

Two other groups also contributed to the early development of this book through their engagement with the material, their questions, and their stimulating ideas—the Sunday morning adult class at the Dayspring church (Edmond, OK) and the Wednesday evening Bible class at the Quail Springs church of Christ (Oklahoma City). In addition, others offered opportunities for me to preach or lecture on this topic and gave helpful feedback and encouragement: the 5th and Main church of Christ (Woodward, OK), the Northwest Expositor's Seminar (Portland, OR), the Caverns Road church of Christ (Marianna, Fl), the Fairmont Park church of Christ (Midland, TX), and the Hope church of Christ (Abilene, TX). To each of these I express my thanks.

I also want to thank Dr. Curt Niccum and Dr. Jeanene Reese, my colleagues at Oklahoma Christian University and Abilene Christian

University respectively, for their close reading of the manuscript. Their probing questions and attention to detail have improved this text greatly and saved me from many embarrassing lapses. And a final word of thanks to David Chisholm, my graduate assistant at ACU, who capably assisted with many details in the final stages of this manuscript and relieved other time pressures that enabled me to complete the work.

Those familiar with scholarship on prophetic literature will recognize my dependence upon a seminal essay by Norman Habel, "The Form and Significance of the Call Narratives" (ZAW 77 [1965]: 297-323). His analysis of the pattern of a call narrative varies somewhat from my own (his is a bit more complex, mine more simplistic); nonetheless my approach stems from his work.

Finally, I dedicate this book to the three people who have surrounded me with their presence and love throughout my writing. To my son and daughter, David and T'auna in gratitude for all the sacrifices you have made to make this project possible–from school days in Denver to all those trips going to teach and preach. You are my heroes. And I dedicate this work to the love of my life, Pam. In response to God's call in the midst of circumstances no one would ever choose, she has lived out the message of God's call to Abraham and Sarah: trust the Lord–especially when the call seems to make no sense. May I and all who read this book be as faithful.

Glenn Pemberton
Abilene, September 2006

Table of Contents

chapter 1

Is He Calling Me?

People called by God—their stories stand at the intersection of every major crisis or turning point in Scripture. A flood is coming to destroy the world; God calls Noah. God embarks on a plan to undo the growing problem of sin, so He commissions Abraham and Sarah. When their descendants find themselves enslaved to a cruel oppressor, God summons Moses. When they face military attack, God calls upon Joshua, then Deborah, Gideon, and Samson, just to name a few. And then there are the prophets, many of whom retell spectacular stories of calling: Samuel and the unfamiliar voice deep in the night, Isaiah and his vision of the Lord enthroned in the temple, Jeremiah protesting that he is too young for this, and Ezekiel—with whatever it was that he saw and ate!

God's call is no minor theme tucked away in a few obscure biblical texts. Rather, from Abraham and Sarah in Ur of the Chaldees to Peter on the shores of Galilee, from Moses on the side of Sinai to Saul on the road to Damascus, and from Isaiah's vision in Jerusalem to John's vision on Patmos, stories of God's call upon the lives of His people leap from the text. Further, most of these stories stand as pivot points for longer and even more famous stories. Everything changes for human history when God calls Abraham and Sarah and the story of Israel begins. The fate of Israel hangs in the balance as God speaks to Moses from the burning bush. And Paul's call on the road to Damascus alters the course of Christianity.

These are not unfamiliar stories and yet, the idea of "calling" that constitutes the essence of these narratives is unfamiliar to many. We know these stories well, but we struggle to know what we are to do with them beyond a resource for reconstructing the longer story. What does God's call to people like Gideon, Barak, or Ezekiel have to do with us? God may have called them, but what relevance does that have for my life? Some may point out the lessons these call narratives teach us about God: God's sovereignty, God's responsiveness to human needs, and God's way of using people to accomplish tasks on earth. But what about the idea of "calling" itself? How does God call people in these texts? What prepares or qualifies an individual to receive God's call? Eventually we come around to the central question for how these texts relate to our lives: Does God still call people today? We struggle with how to answer and for good reason find ourselves torn in two directions.

My father-in-law, Harvey (Red), grew up in Gulfport, Mississippi in a Christian tradition, but outside the Stone-Campbell movement. After graduation from high school he joined the Air Force and eventually landed in Midland, Texas among the churches of Christ. One consequence of raising a family in Midland with his own extended family back in Gulfport was the annual pilgrimage home to visit grandparents, aunts, uncles, and cousins—a lengthy trip that usually led to spending the weekend, including a Sunday morning in Gulfport. One particular Sunday, as was the custom, Red and his family got up and went to the local church of Christ while the rest of the family went to his old home church. This year, however, a dilemma faced him upon his arrival at church; he was the only male present.

There was only one viable solution to the crisis. Harvey proceeded to teach the Bible class and conduct the worship assembly. He led all the prayers, read Scriptures, served the communion, took up the collection, attempted to lead the singing (by his own acknowledgement, not his gift), made the announcements, and to the great delight of his daughters, he preached the sermon.

The after-church reunion back at the home place found two excited young girls proudly announcing "Daddy preached! Daddy preached!" A revelation that caught the attention of Harvey's brother, a lay-ordained pastor at the family's church who immediately asked him THE question: "Why Harvey, I didn't know! When did you receive your call to preach?" To which Red replied, "When I got to the building and they asked me." Not to be put off, Harvey's brother began to recount his own story of calling. It was a Saturday night and he was drawing up his bath water, leaning over the tub to put the stopper in the drain when God called him to preach. To which, Harvey interrupted, "Sounds to me like you just pulled a muscle!"

> We would never deny God's ability or freedom to do anything; we are just not so sure about contemporary claims of personal calling and those who make them....

Such a jesting, questioning, skeptical attitude toward divine calling is fairly common among members of the churches of Christ. We would never deny God's ability or freedom to do anything; we are just not so sure about contemporary claims of personal calling and those who make them, a reluctance that stems from our roots. One chromosome in our spiritual DNA as children of the Stone-Campbell heritage is a deep suspicion of "a personal call." In fact, the trajectory set by our spiritual ancestors was in sharp reaction to two common practices of "calling" in the early 1800's. First, Calvinistic teachings of the time emphasized the limited scope of God's atonement; not everyone was called to salvation, only the elect. Worse, a person did not know if he was a member of the elect unless he had experienced a personal and visible "call" from God. As a result, the earliest use of mourner's benches (the precursor to coming forward in response to an invitation song) came into practice for people convinced and convicted by the preaching, but who had not yet received or experienced a "call." They came forward, waited, and hoped for a call that would confirm their status as one of God's elect for salvation.

Campbell and Stone (later) fought against this Calvinistic concept of calling, arguing instead from texts such as II Thessalonians that God calls all people to salvation through the proclamation of the gospel. Here, Paul writes to the church that God "called you through our proclamation of the good news" (2:13-14). One does not need to await the experience of a call; God has already issued it in the preaching about Christ. And this call, Peter claims, is "for you, for your children, and for all who are far away, everyone whom the Lord our God calls to him" (Acts 2:39). So instead of waiting for a call from God, Campbell argued that a convicted believer should act in such a way as to receive the call God has already extended.

A second practice to which Stone and Campbell responded was the special calling of clergy to an ordained status in the church. In their day, many denominations required a candidate for ordination to recount his experience of God's call to the office of a pastor. If a candidate had no such experience, the church would not ordain him. Campbell countered that the early church did not recognize such an ordained, "called" clergy. All Christians are a "chosen race, a royal priesthood, a holy nation" (I Peter 2:9). The New Testament knows nothing of a clergy-laity division with a special class of called priests officiating over non-called "lay" members. Consequently, two distinctive doctrines emerged in early preaching among churches of Christ: 1) God calls all people to salvation through the gospel, and 2) God calls all those saved to ministry in the church.

Our spiritual ancestry, then, has led us to be suspicious of any claim to a special call from God. Certainly, God has called many servants throughout the course of history. We would never deny God's right or ability to do so then or now. God can call whomever God wishes when God pleases. But we are, after all, talking about spiritual giants, called people such as Moses, Isaiah, Jeremiah, and Paul. It stands against our spiritual DNA and seems a bit presumptuous, even arrogant, to claim a "called" place among such heroes of the faith. So we hesitate when we hear such a claim—and would never make such an assertion for ourselves.

This strand of DNA remains strong among many, but not all. For others, the two centuries since Stone and Campbell have weakened this genetic trait; attitudes about divine calling have changed and continue to do so. Whether such change is appropriate will be addressed in the course of this study. For now the point is a simple observation: many members of the churches of Christ no longer share our traditional skepticism or rejection of personal calling. To be sure, we still reject the Calvinistic idea of calling and the special call of an ordained clergy. But some are more receptive to those who make claims about God's call on their lives to special service and are acutely concerned about discerning God's call upon our own lives.

One evidence of this renewed concern is the popularity of Annie Herring's song "There's a Stirring":

Verse One:	There's a stirring deep within me,
	Could it be my time has come?
	When I see my gracious Savior,
	Face to face when all is done.
	Is that his voice I am hearing,
	"Come away, my precious one."
	Is He calling me? Is He calling me?
Chorus:	I will rise up,
	I'll rise up.
	And bow down,
	And lay my crown
	At His wounded feet.

This song is majestic, especially when sung with an audience of two thousand or more passionate young people. My students love this song and I like it too, but I must say that it is morbid. Literally, "There's a Stirring" is a song about death (or perhaps some concept of a rapture). The opening lines pose the question, "could it be my time has come?" my time to face my Savior when "all is done." The stirring to which this song refers is an inner uncertainty about whether my time to die has come, and thus the writer poses the question: "Is he calling me?" This reading of the song is confirmed by the second verse, not sung in any congregational arrangements that I have heard.

Verse Two: Could it be the gates of heaven,
                      Swinging open just for me?
                      Could it be my Lord is coming,
                      Coming now to set me free?
                      Is that His voice I am hearing,
                      "Come away, my precious one."
                      Is He calling me? Is He calling me?

My training as a historical-critical exegete or interpreter makes this "deathly" meaning of the song clear to me; I could not sing it without this understanding. But I am equally convinced that some of my students are not thinking about death when they sing this song. Instead, they exercise something of a reader-response method in singing. Unbound from any original intent of the author, they seize upon key lyrics and fill these with their own meanings. Here, they seize upon the question "Is he calling me?" and ask not whether they are about to die, but whether God is calling them to special service. They want to know if God is calling, to what God is calling, and how they can recognize this call.

My suspicions of this understanding of the song were recently confirmed when a former student sent me a Portuguese version of

"There's a Stirring." Back-translated from the Portuguese into English, the first verse now reads:

> A voice calls me whispering in the depth of my being
> This calling is insistent, and I need to respond
> God stirs my soul, I have to obey;
> It says, "Come to me."
> I am coming Lord, I'm coming

In this version, explicitly, the call is no longer about death but surrender to the will of God for my life, whatever God's will or call may be.

This reader-response method to singing and especially to singing songs about calling is not new. While drafting this chapter I visited a congregation that sang the older (1937) hymn "I'll Be Listening"

Verse One:	When the Savior calls I will answer,
	When he calls for me I will hear;
	When the Savior calls I will answer,
	I'll be somewhere list'ning for my name.
Chorus:	I'll be somewhere list'ning,
	I'll be somewhere list'ning,
	I'll be somewhere list'ning for my name.
	(repeat once)
Verse Two:	If my heart is right when He calls me,
	If my heart is right I will hear;
	If my heart is right when He calls me,
	I'll be somewhere list'ning for my name.
Verse Three:	If my robe is white when he calls me,
	If my robe is white I will hear;

If my robe is white when he calls me,
I'll be somewhere list'ning for my name.

Again, the original meaning of the song is about death or the second coming of Christ; with a pure heart and white robe we await the call of God to a life beyond. And yet, I would estimate only half of the assembly sang the song with such an understanding, The other half was anxious to keep their hearts and robes pure so that they could hear the Savior's call upon their lives here and now.

So we find ourselves in somewhat of a bind. On the one side, our genetic predisposition leads us to be skeptical about calling while on the other side a resurgence of interest is leading to a greater openness to the idea. This study responds to and exists in the midst of this tension. Obviously in this short work we will not resolve all the tensions or questions about calling, but I do hope we can resolve a few and in the process allow Scripture to work in our lives in fresh ways. Of course Scripture is the most reliable resource for reflection on the concept of calling. And on this topic we are not left in a lurch for pertinent texts. Call narratives dot the landscape of the Bible and offer to us a place to come together, read together, and converse with one another about God's call. In what follows we set out on a trek to revisit these many well-known stories and perhaps a few that are not so well known. But in both cases we come with a set of questions we may not have considered before, questions about God's calling on the lives of the people in the text and God's calling upon our lives.

At the risk of immediate misunderstanding, I do need to address briefly two common misconceptions about calling in the Bible before we close this introduction. First, while God's call sometimes came upon people in mysterious and even miraculous ways (e.g., Isaiah, Moses), this was not always the case. As we will see, God called Joshua primarily through the work of Moses, just as God called Timothy through Paul selecting and taking Timothy with him on his third missionary journey (Acts 16:1-3). In much the same way God calls elders ("the Holy Spirit has made you overseers" [Acts 20:28]) through the church's process of identification and selection (Titus 1:5-9; I Timothy 3:1-7). There is no question that Joshua, Timothy, and the elders were all called by God, but they received their call through the mediation of others, including the church. Thus, God's call does not necessarily require a mysterious or miraculous event.

Second, God's call often summons a person to speak on God's behalf, to be a prophet or preacher (e.g., Jeremiah, Ezekiel). But this is by no means the only commission to which God calls people in the Bible. God called Noah to build a boat and Moses (at least at first) to involve himself in the politics of justice. Joshua was summoned to be a military and political leader. And God called others such as Abraham, Sarah, Mary, and Zechariah to trust Him to do what

> **God's call does not necessarily require a mysterious or miraculous event.**

He promised to do in their lives. God's calling is not limited to preaching or prophesy in the Bible.

Now, with some awareness of the history of this topic in the Stone-Campbell movement that continues to influence our thinking, with a recognition of both the traditional and newer attitudes toward divine calling, and with this brief corrective that divine calling in Scripture is not limited to miraculous means or prophetic purposes, we now turn to consider the form or pattern of call narratives in the Bible as a prelude to engaging the individual stories of what happens when God calls.

Discussion Questions:

1. Examine the list of people called by God included in this chapter. Identify others God called in the Bible. How did God call them? To what tasks did God call these servants? How did these calls and tasks fulfill God's purposes in each situation?

2. Brainstorm about songs that use the terms "call" or "calling." Examine the lyrics of these songs. What appears to be the original idea of the author? What have you thought while singing them? Compare your responses to the author's intent—is it the same or different? What accounts for the differences, if any?

3. Have you ever known anyone who claimed to have a special calling from God? How was it received by others? What was their story? How did you feel about their claim? Why?

4. On a scale of 1 to 10 (with 10 being the strongest) how would you rate the strength of your spiritual DNA regarding calling? What effect would you say that the Stone-Campbell heritage has on your attitudes? Explain.

5. What do you hope to learn from this study of the call narratives? What questions do you have about this subject at this point in your reading?

chapter 2

Reading the Call Narratives
Genesis 24:1-61; Judges 6:11-24

Without notice a friend interrupts our breakfast, blindfolds us, spins us around in circles, and whisks us away in a taxi. The next thing we know our friend pulls us out of the cab and leads us into a building where we sit for a moment, still blindfolded, and hear the words: "Dearly beloved, we are gathered here today in the sight of God and these witnesses," before we are escorted back to the waiting taxi.

The driver pulls away and after winding through city streets, she stops. Again, our host opens the door and leads us by the hand into another building, down a corridor, and through what sounds like large squeaky doors. We sit just long enough to hear a stern voice at the front of the room ask, "Do you swear to tell the truth, the whole truth, and nothing but the truth?" Then it is back to the taxi for a more tranquil ride that seems to lead outside of the city, although we cannot be sure. As we get out of the cab, our suspicions are confirmed. The noise of traffic is muffled in the distance and we catch the distinctive scent of the country. Our host, still refusing our sight, leads us a few paces to a place where we remain standing and after a few moments of silence followed by the shuffling of many feet we hear the words, "Beau Bailey was born on June 8, 1926, in Marianna, Florida, and passed from this life on..." But again, we hear no more because our host has snatched us away. We return home where, thankfully, our friend removes our blindfold. The whirlwind trip has left us a bit exhausted, but oddly, not at all confused about our experience.

Pause for a moment and take a quiz about the day: Where did our adventure lead? Can you identify the three places and events that we visited? Beyond what we heard, what else could you surmise about what took place before and after you left each place? Despite the fact that we were blindfolded, disoriented, and only allowed to hear a few words at each stop, we know much about the events we dropped in on. Of course our first stop, with the words "dearly beloved we are gathered here today in the presence of God and these witnesses," was a wedding. And this recognition embarrasses us because we realize that we were tardy. Before the minister (again we speculate with confidence) spoke these words the ceremony had already begun with music, processionals, and prayer. Moreover, even though we were whisked away after hearing these few words we can reconstruct the remainder of the ceremony with a fair degree of certainty. As we drive away we can envision the wedding sermon, the vows, rings, perhaps a unity candle, prayers, wedding music, a pronouncement of marriage, a kiss, presentation of the couple, and a grand recessional. We may have missed the wedding, but we still know all this. We only wonder what type of food we missed at the reception.

The second stop, we guessed correctly, was a court of law. And again, although we only caught a few words (a bailiff swearing in a witness) and could not see a thing, we can reconstruct the scene in our mind: a judge, a court reporter, a defendant, his attorney, a prosecuting attorney, a jury, and a few interested people in the audience. It's more difficult to know how far along the trial has proceeded or the nature of the case—civil or criminal. At the very least the attorneys have completed their opening statements and are now presenting evidence and witnesses. Later, after we left, they will summarize their cases to the jury in final arguments, the jury will deliberate in private, reach an agreement, and then pronounce a verdict. We may have only been in the room for a matter of seconds, but it is clear in our imagination what has happened and will happen.

Our final stop was indeed a final stop, at least for Mr. Beau Bailey who was being laid to rest at a local cemetery. The people at this event would have been dressed more somberly, quite a contrast to the earlier wedding party. Had we been allowed to stay longer we would have heard something about Mr. Bailey's life, his accomplishments, his family, words from Scripture (perhaps even Psalm 23), and a prayer. We would know or be able to predict many of these things here and at our other stops despite the fact that we were blindfolded, had no idea where we had been taken, and heard only a few passing words at each locale. A word of self-congratulation is in order; we've done quite well with a very limited amount of information.

How did we know all this? What enabled us to make such lengthy deductions from such a small amount of data? Two things made this possible: 1) the common way in which these events take place in our culture, and 2) our familiarity with these patterns. Weddings in Western Christian culture follow a traditional form or pattern (in other cultures weddings follow other patterns), as do court trials, funerals, graduations, inaugurations, and other important life events.

As a result of the traditional patterns and our familiarity with them, we know how to "read" these events. At a wedding, for example, we know what to notice, what does not merit our attention, and what to appreciate because, despite their common appearances, no two weddings are exactly the same. Every couple places their unique stamp on their wedding by working with the traditional patterns, tweaking the expected, and occasionally even flaunting the norms. The key to recognizing what they have done, however, is prior knowledge of the common pattern. A person who attends a wedding for the first time is unaware of the customs, and thus is prone to notice everything except what the couple has done to make their wedding unique. He may marvel at the matching formal attire, the bride's white dress, the beautiful flowers, and the many symbolic actions: giving away the bride, the unity candle, the kiss. And yet, a first timer will miss the slight or not so slight ways the couple has altered all of these things to fit their unique personality and love story.

Our novice, for example, would not have thought twice about the wedding I performed in which the bridesmaids included a six foot-six inch "bridesman" standing on the bride's side and the grooms-men included a five foot-two inch "groomswoman" standing on the groom's side. Nor would a novice have noticed that at my niece's wedding the unity candle was replaced by "unity sand." Instead of lighting a candle, the bride and groom poured separate vials of colored sand into a common vase, creating a beautiful mixture of color and design. But again, our first time wedding attendee would have only known that we were outdoors in the midst of a drought with a strict ban against outdoor fires; he would have never caught that a substitution had taken place.

The point to all this is simple and helpful to our reading of Scripture. First, important events in societies tend to take place in typical, repeatable patterns. Second, if we are to interpret or read these events or texts with insight, we need to be familiar with the patterns. We need to be able to see what is normal and what is unusual in any particular instance of a common event. Otherwise our reading may miss the subtle and overt variations that direct us to the author's special concerns.

Like us, ancient Near Eastern societies such as Israel also had common patterns of behavior and speech that originated in life settings: laments (from funeral dirges), judgment speeches (from trials), and psalms of thanksgiving (from thanksgiving sacrifices in the temple) just to name a few. Each of these events or types of speech followed typical patterns because—well, that's just the way it was done in their society. Ancient Israelites did not lack imagination or creativity any more than a modern bride and groom. Rather, they followed the conventional ways of doing and saying things and made them uniquely their own by introducing variations within the patterns.

In addition to laments, psalms of thanksgiving, and judgment oracles, ancient Israel had other culturally conditioned ways of doing things, including a form or pattern for how a master called a servant to a special task; what we refer to here as a call narrative. Genesis 24 offers an excellent case study of such a call narrative and its typical components. At first glance, this chapter seems eccentric; it is a long chapter that is supposed to be about Isaac's marriage to Rebekah, but the actual marriage scene consists of only one verse, the last verse out of sixty seven (24:67). Of greater concern to the author, and our interest here, is the way in which Abraham calls his servant to the task of finding a bride for his son—a call narrative retold twice in the chapter, first by the narrator (24:1-9) and then by the servant as he tells his tale to Rebekah's family (24:33-49).

To begin, a crisis looms in the background of Genesis 24. Sarah has just died and been buried in the land of promise (23:1-20) and Abraham is old—very old, the narrator stresses (24:1). Isaac, who is now 40 years old (25:20), is not yet married and the prospects seem grim. Even grimmer is the overall situation. Isaac is the covenant child who is supposed to fulfill and continue God's promise to Abraham and Sarah that their offspring would be as numerous as the stars in the sky. Isaac needs a wife, the right wife. Time is running out for Abraham.

Abraham summons the attention of his most trusted servant from the midst of his daily routine. The servant neither seeks nor expects such a special calling. Once Abraham has his attention, Abraham indicates the gravity of the situation by asking the servant to pledge an especially serious oath ("put your hand under my thigh" [24:2]). At this point, in his own retelling, the servant explains his relationship with Abraham (24:34) and the situation back home that has led to his calling or commission (24:35-36).

Next, Abraham issues his commission: "You will not get a wife for my son from the daughters of the Canaanites, among whom I live, but will go to my country and to my kindred and get a wife for my son Isaac" (24:3-4). Abraham's call includes a clear objective for the servant: go get the right wife for my son. But in this call the servant becomes more than a mere messenger for the master. He becomes Abraham's personal representative in all matters pertaining to the task, the acquisition of a wife for Isaac. Abraham invests him with both responsibility and authority to act on his behalf and complete his commission.

The servant objects. What if I go, find the right woman, but she is unwilling to come to this land? In such a circumstance should I then take Isaac back to your homeland to marry her (24:5, retold in 24:39)? His objection points out an obvious and probable difficulty with the commission. The servant cannot control the response of the bride-to-be or her family. She may balk at the idea of leaving the security of homeland and family. What then?

Abraham is not surprised, flustered, or angered by his servant's objection; a servant's right to voice the obvious problems seems par for the course. Instead, Abraham responds with words of reassurance. His servant must not take Isaac out of the land because it is this land, the land of Canaan that God has promised to him and to Isaac (24:6-7). If the woman refuses, then the servant is free of the obligations of Abraham's call, but under no circumstance is he to take Isaac out of the land (24:8). Significantly, when the servant's retelling of the story gets to this point he adds two things. First, he says that his master Abraham also reassured him that the Lord would send an angel with him to make his way successful (24:40). Second, the servant retells his own request for a sign from God earlier that day at the well. He asked God to identify the correct woman by means of a test. The servant would ask a woman who came to the well, "Please give me a little water from your jar to drink," and the woman God selected would be the one who responded, "Drink, and I will draw for your camels also" (24:43-44). As requested, God identifies Rebekah as the right woman and shows favor to the servant by means of this sign.

After further negotiations, the servant arranges the marriage and overcomes the family's reluctance for Rebekah to leave their land. Soon Isaac and Rebekah marry, but do not particularly live happily ever after. And here, we take our leave of their story to reflect on the pattern of calling exemplified by this narrative. Abraham's call of his servant follows a basic six step procedure or pattern: 1) a crisis is on the horizon, 2) the master summons the attention of a servant from his or her daily routine, 3) the master provides some explanation of the need or reason for the commission and stresses the existing relationship between himself and the servant, 4) the master commissions the servant to a specific task with the necessary authority to represent the master in all ways pertaining to the task, 5) the servant states an objection that voices an obvious or likely problem with the commission, and 6) the master responds to the objection with words of assurance that usually include a restatement of the commission and, in instances of God's call, offers a sign of divine favor. Compare this pattern to Abraham's call of his servant in Genesis 24.

The Pattern	Genesis 24
Crisis	The heir of the promise is unmarried and must acquire the right wife.
Summons	Abraham summons his servant to attention from the midst of his daily routine.
Introduction	Abraham, and especially the servant in his retelling, explains the master/servant relationship and the reason for this call.
Commission	Abraham commissions his servant to get the right wife for his son and authorizes him as his representative.
Objection	The servants voices the problem with the commission: What if the right woman will not come back with him to marry Isaac?
Reassurance	Abraham reassures his servant that God will send an angel ahead of him and the servant gains a sign from God that denotes the Lord's favor.

The call of Abraham's servant fits this outline not because it is contrived or even derived from this text, but because this was the common way for a master to call a servant to any special task in ancient Israel. This is the way it was done in society and thus, the way in which Abraham's call upon his servant takes place and is retold. An ancient audience would have expected no less.

A second instance of this pattern may be observed in Judges 6, the call of Gideon. Here, the continual invasion of Midianites and others has left Israel impoverished and scurrying for shelter in the mountains (6:1-6). God summons Gideon to attention by means of an angel who interrupts his daily routine of threshing wheat in a winepress (to keep it from the Midianites, 6:11-13). In an unusual move Gideon, rather than the angel, responds with the introductory words that describe the background for this call. Gideon asks how this person (not yet identified as an angel by Gideon) can claim God is with anyone in Israel? God was once with Israel in mighty and miraculous ways, but not now. Now the Lord has abandoned His people to the Midianites (6:13). God's commission follows Gideon's questions: "Go in this might of yours and deliver Israel from the hand of Midian; I hereby commission you" (6:14). To which Gideon immediately objects, "But sir, how can I deliver Israel? My clan is the weakest in Manasseh, and I am the least in my family" (6:15). Finally, God reassures Gideon that He will be with him and that he will succeed against Midian (6:16); a sign of divine favor, on Gideon's request, follows (6:17-24).

Once we recognize this traditional form or pattern for calling a servant in ancient Israel, we are in a better position to read the call stories and catch their unique features and message. Like a wedding, we may quickly identify common elements that we expect to see. For example, there is nothing particularly noteworthy in Gideon or Abraham's servant voicing an objection; this was an expected part of any calling. But, we may also notice parts of the pattern that have been changed, expanded, or omitted in a particular story. In upcoming chapters we will be struck by the fact that Moses objects not once but five times to his call, while Joshua offers no objection at all. Isaiah responds with "Here I am, send me" before he knows the content of his commission; and Jonah just runs. In all these cases and others, the changes to the typical form of the call narrative offer vital clues to the writer's message.

Reading special events such as wedding, trials, and funerals, and reading a call narrative, then, are not all that different. Aware of the tradition, the way things are supposed to happen with this event in this culture, we recognize the slight and not so slight departures from the norm—and these point us toward the unique message of the biblical writer. So, the traditional pattern of an ancient Near Eastern call narrative provides a new, clarifying lens through which we may examine these stories, a task to which we now turn.

Discussion Questions:

1. Reconsider the list of call narratives that you compiled (from the Discussion Questions for chapter 1). Do these stories fit the pattern of a call narrative as set out by this chapter? How do they vary? Why do you suppose they depart from the typical pattern?

2. Both ancient Israel and contemporary society use common forms or patterns in events such as weddings and funerals. What other contemporary events follow traditional patterns? Describe the patterns in these events. Why do you think we do this?

3. The author claims that the servant had the right or was even expected to object to the commission of a call. From your list of call narratives, how many people object to God's call? What was their objection or reason? Which objections are reasonable and which are not? Where do you draw the line between a reasonable objection and stubborn obstinacy?

4. Discuss how the call is almost always a test of faith for the one being called.

chapter 3

Abraham and Sarah:
The First Lesson for the Called

Genesis 12—22

Paul Marcarelli is a thirty-something celebrity from New York City, although few are likely to know him by name. He is the Test Man, the fellow who walks about in the Verizon Wireless phone commercials asking the same question over and over: "Can you hear me now?" and then after a brief pause replies, "Good." That's Marcarelli's job; travel all over the country, set up the cameras in exotic locations, stride across the screen, say six words, and then call it a day. "Can you hear me now?" What a great job! "Good."

Our teenaged daughter lives as if this question were the most important issue in life. Some years ago I questioned our family's need to purchase a new answering machine on the basis that our daughter immediately answered every call on the first ring (and every call was for her anyway). Why buy an answering machine when we already have an answering service? I lost that battle and the next. Some time later my wife talked me into buying a package deal of three cordless phones in one system. The rationale was that we could disperse the phones throughout the house and so be able to find a phone when it rang. I will admit that this purchase did resolve our frequent phone searches. If I needed a phone I just went to my daughter's room where every cordless phone migrated at the speed of sound.

She cannot tolerate a weak phone signal or static on the line, much less a dropped call due to a weak battery. So, if one cordless phone began to fade, our package deal enabled her to run to the next room, grab another phone and continue the conversation back in her room. I used to wonder why any family would need more than one phone in a house; now I don't give it a second thought. Of course these days we have graduated to cell phones, text messaging, and call waiting despite my protest why we need these contraptions. "Can you hear me now?" is our family motto—and probably yours too.

It would appear that many Christians are likewise convinced that this question is of utmost importance to God, as if God is pacing back and forth in heaven nervously asking again and again: Can they hear me now? And so, we conclude, a primary Christian concern should be listening for, identifying, and discerning the call of God. We imagine that these are primary human tasks while God helplessly waits to discover if we can clearly hear His voice. God places the call but people must be ready to receive the call, recognize it when it comes, and make sure that they have a clear connection to hear the voice of God. All this responsibility, so the thinking goes, is on our shoulders. As a result, many Christians devote considerable time and energy to trying to discern the call of God on their lives and then to helping others learn how to recognize God's call for themselves. So the question "Can they hear me now?" transitions to "How do I discern the call of God in my life?" And this question becomes the first and driving question for discussions of calling.

While I do not deny the validity of this question or the sincerity of those who ask it, this is simply not a vital topic in the biblical stories of calling. Yes, Samuel's call raises questions about discerning the voice of God but, as we will see, all of the other stories make the assumption that God is the one responsible for acquiring a person's attention and making himself heard. Even in Samuel's story, it is

God who takes the initiative for getting through, not Samuel. In the biblical text establishing the connection is God's business, not a human concern, and God can and will do whatever is necessary to summon the attention of a servant and call him to special work. God can light a bush (Moses), strike a person blind (Saul), or continue to call out in the night (Samuel) if that's what it takes. But you and I can relax, "Can they hear me now?" has never been God's concern. Instead, the biblical call stories begin with another, more fundamental concern.

> **God can and will do whatever is necessary to summon the attention of a servant and call him to special work.**

Genesis 1-11 presents the tragic tale of a good creation gone horribly bad. In Genesis 1 everything is good. Repeatedly, God pauses at the end of each day of creation, looks and sees that "it was good" (e.g., 1:10). This evaluative summary begins on day three and climaxes on day six when God observes everything He had made and concludes that "it was very good" (1:31). The same theme of a good creation extends into Genesis 2 as well. Here, however, the emphasis is on the goodness of the relationships that God has established. The relationship between the humans and the ecosystem is good; humans tend the garden and the garden provides for them. The relationship between the male and the female is good; they are made for one another, cling to one another, and are naked but not ashamed. And the relationship between God and the humans could not be better; God is responsive to and has provided for every human need. No question about it, God's creation was indeed very good.

But it went very wrong. In Genesis 3 every relationship unravels. Rather than trust their creator, the couple views God as a micromanager who is holding them back from the good life. They take life into their own hands, wreck their relationship with God, and as a direct result damage every other relationship. The man and woman no longer trust each other but are consumed with blame and shame. God ejects them from the garden for their own good and curses the ground. And while God is far from giving up on a relationship with these people, it would appear that the bond has been irreparably harmed. The loss of trust is difficult to recover.

In subsequent stories in Genesis 4-11 the problems just get worse, to the point that in an excruciating reversal of God's exclamation that creation was "very good," God now sees that "the wickedness of humankind was great in the earth, and that every inclination of the thoughts of their heart was only evil continually. And the Lord was sorry that he had made humankind on the earth, and it grieved him to his heart" (Genesis 6:5-6). From divine joy to divine grief, creation has indeed gone very wrong.

What is a God to do with a good creation gone bad? To be sure, in Genesis 3-11 God responds in numerous ways to curb the problem. But nothing works. God may exile the couple from the garden, banish Cain to wandering, destroy the world and start over again, or confuse the unity of the people so they cannot cooperate in self-defeating projects, but none of these steps resolves the ultimate problem. Sin continues to spread, intensify, and worsen. At the end of Genesis 11 the key question for God and the reader is potently without an answer: what is a God to do with such a promising start that has turned into such a mess?

God's response is to issue a call to an unsuspecting and unlikely couple: Abraham (Abram) and Sarah (Sarai).

> Now the Lord said to Abram, "Go from your country and your kindred and your father's house to the land that I will show you. I will make of you a great nation, and I will bless you, and make your name great, so that you will be a blessing. I will bless those who bless you, and the one who curs-

es you I will curse; and in you all the families of the earth shall be blessed... to your offspring I will give this land. (Genesis 12:1-3,7a)

Compared to the typical form of a call narrative, we might wonder if this story really belongs in the same category. For example, while we certainly have a major crisis looming in the background (Genesis 1-11) this story lays little stress on the summons to attention. In a classic case of understatement the text simply says "the Lord said to Abram" with no hint of the surprise or disruption this summons had on Abraham and Sarah's life. Nor at this point does the Lord provide any introductory words of explanation to preface the commission. And Abraham does not offer a single objection in Genesis 12:1-9. Is this really a call narrative and, if so, how are we to understand these variations from how things are supposed to happen?

I do believe we are dealing with a call narrative in this text, but this calling is not as concise or compact as most of the other stories we will study. Instead of a few verses or a single chapter that recounts Abraham's calling, what we have is an extended call story that spans eleven chapters (Genesis 12-22) and many years. This expansion is unusual, but nonetheless a call narrative. God does summon Abraham's attention in the midst of his daily routine. How God got his attention is of no interest to the story, nor is the shock this summons must have been to Abraham and Sarah. They were not searching for a call from God. In fact, later we are made aware that before God called Abraham, he and his family served other gods (Joshua 24:2). No wonder God's initial call to Abraham offers no explanatory word that stresses their existing relationship. There was probably no prior relationship, at least not from Abraham's perspective. In later reiterations of His call God will explain more of the situation and attest to their growing relationship, but that must necessarily come later.

Here at the beginning, God simply explains the plan He has for Abraham and Sarah's life. In simple terms, God promises to do three things for them: 1) give them many descendants (a great nation), 2) give them much land (that a great nation will require), and 3) through them work a blessing for all the nations of the earth. Exactly how this plan will resolve the crisis of sin is ambiguous and left unexplained. What is clear is that God takes on the responsibility to deal with the problems of Genesis 3-11 through Abraham and Sarah. God will give descendants, land, and a blessing to the world through them. God takes on the burden of resolving this crisis. So then, if this is what God is planning to do, what is the commission to Abraham and Sarah? What are they supposed to do?

God's call to Abraham and Sarah in Genesis 12 consists of a single word: Go (12:1). Go from your home country, your people and family; go to the land that I will show you. Just go—and for a couple who live beyond the Euphrates and serve other gods that's enough to ask. Our mobile society with families scattered miles, states, and even oceans apart will find it difficult to imagine the radical nature of this call for them. Homeland, family, and the family gods were a person's security in the ancient world. Without these one was vulnerable, defenseless, a wanderer without many legal rights.

With one word God commissions Abraham and Sarah to an entirely new life, and God promises to provide the security, a new large family, and a new homeland. All that Sarah and Abraham must do is go, pack up, and set out. And of course, there's the catch. Above all else, for this couple to accept this call they must decide whether they can trust this God. They must have faith that the Lord will do what He has promised to do in their lives, and their trust must be great enough to risk their lives. It boils down to one question: Will they trust the God who calls them?

While Abraham offers no initial objection to God's call, he does protest later in the story. God has asked Abraham and Sarah to go in faith that God will give them numerous descendants. The problem, of course, is that Sarah is barren (Genesis 11:30) and the only fertility clinic available to them is their slave Hagar, who is not on the divine HMO plan! Several times Abraham brings this rather obvious problem to the Lord's attention. He responds to a vision from God in Genesis 15 by asking, "O Lord God, what will you give me, for I continue childless, and the heir of my house is Eliezer of Damascus?" and pointing out the Lord's failure to this point, "You have given me no offspring, and so a slave born in my house is to be my heir" (15:2-3). Later, after God reiterates the promise of a son to the couple, Abraham falls on his face laughing at the idea and asks himself, "Can a child be born to a man who is a hundred years old? Can Sarah, who is ninety years old, bear a child?" (Genesis 17:17). Even Sarah objects when she overhears a house guest (one of the heavenly visitors, but does she know this?) tell Abraham that Sarah will have a son. She laughs to herself and questions, "After I have grown old, and my husband is old, shall I have pleasure?" (18:12). Both Abraham and Sarah raise the evident difficulty with the Lord's plan; Sarah is barren, they are both too old—this is crazy.

In the same way Abraham points out the logical flaw with God's promise of land. People are already living there with no plans to move out! Abraham owns not so much as a camping space. So he asks "O Lord God, how am I to know that I shall possess it?" (Genesis 15:8). And on God's third promise, the reader is left to raise objections about how God could possibly work a blessing to the world through this family. More often than not, Abraham and Sarah leave a wake of disaster in their path. The Lord afflicts Pharaoh and his family because of them (Genesis 12:17). Hagar and Ishmael suffer as a result of their actions (Genesis 16:6; 21:8-14). And God plagues Abimelech and his family in Gerar due to Abraham and Sarah (Genesis 20:1-17). One wonders what God was thinking when He called this family to be a blessing to the world.

God's call upon Abraham and Sarah may have been a simple command ("go"), but it strikes at the heart of every calling in every place and time. To accept God's call requires us first to trust the God who calls us to do what He has promised to do in our lives. This struggle to trust becomes a focal point for the duration of Abraham and Sarah's story, where serious obstacles stand between God's promises and reality. Will they trust this God or do they take matters into their own hands? Episode after episode finds them wrestling with this issue. Against God's directive to leave his family, Abraham brings along his nephew Lot and exhibits tremendous concern for his well-being in story after story, perhaps because he thinks Lot may be the only heir he will ever have. Abraham fails to trust the God who calls and pawns off Sarah as his sister not just once, but twice (Genesis 12:10–13:1 and 20:1-7). Sarah and Abraham give up on God to provide a child, decide that Hagar is the only solution and that they had better put things in motion before it is too late (16:1-16). And in every case, the failure to trust further complicates God's call.

The Lord responds to Abraham and Sarah's objections with reassuring words and actions. God knows that this call is not easy to swallow. So in every instance God encourages the couple to trust Him. When Abraham asks how he can know that he will possess the land, God initiates a covenant ceremony (15:9-21) in which God further explains His plan to Abraham (15:13-16) and binds himself to the promise "To your descendants I give this land" (15:18). When Abraham questions God about having his own son, God reassures him that he and Sarah will have a son of their own (15:4; 17:19) and that his descendants will be as numerous as the stars in the sky (15:5). When the couple laugh at the absurdity of having a baby at their age, God reassures them: "Is anything too wonderful for the Lord? At the set time I will return to you, in due season, and Sarah shall have a son" (18:14). God urges this beleaguered pair to trust Him to do what He has promised to do with their lives.

And so it happens that in the middle of many objections and frequent failures to trust this God who calls, that a single verse stands out. After one of his more poignant objections that this God who called him has not yet provided a son, and after God's reassurance to Abraham that he will have his own heir and many descendants, the text reads: "And he believed the Lord; and the Lord reckoned it to him as righteousness" (15:6). That's all the Lord asked of Abraham, just trust me, and he did. He placed his faith and his life in the hands of the God who called him.

> **The first lesson of calling is not how to discern or hear the voice of God.... the first and foremost issue is trust.**

The first lesson of calling is not how to discern or hear the voice of God. Abraham and Sarah heard and understood the call of God on their lives—and how they heard it or how God got through to them is not even a passing issue in the text. Instead, the first and foremost issue is trust. Will we trust the God who calls us? Will we step out in faith to do what God has set before us? Everything hinges on this question. God asks Abraham and Sarah, Trust me—that I know what I am doing, especially when it may not look like it. Trust me that the success of this plan is up to me, not you. Trust me that when everything points against my promises and there is still no child, no land, and no blessing, that I will do what I have promised. What I need you to do is to be patient, give me the time and space to do my work. Your task is not to make it happen but to be faithful to my call on your life: Go and trust the God who has called you.

Discussion Questions:

1. Do you agree or disagree that God is not concerned with the question "Can they hear me now?" Why or why not?

2. Genesis 1-11 describes the crisis that prompts God to call Abraham and Sarah. Other than the points the author mentions, what other crises do you see in these chapters? How will God's call to Abraham and Sarah resolve these problems? What does this solution teach us about God? About ourselves?

3. Had you been Abraham how do you think you would react to God's call to leave country and family? Assuming God first spoke to Abraham alone, how do you think he explained this call Sarah? How do you think she might have reacted? How typical or atypical are these responses?

4. Why do you think Abraham and Sarah were willing to embrace the Lord's call on their lives, especially when they had been serving other gods?

5. What was the single greatest obstacle for Abraham and Sarah's trust in the Lord? Explain. What made trusting the Lord so difficult for them? Why is it so difficult for us? For you specifically?

chapter 4

Moses: Tell God I'm Not Available

Exodus 3—4

In the opening chapters of Exodus the family of Israel faced a crisis like none before. To be sure, from Abraham and Sarah to Jacob with his wives and children, Israel's ancestors had dealt with difficulties that endangered their well-being and even their lives. Neighbors sometimes felt threatened by the family's growing strength and wealth, an anxiety that found expression in heated disputes and even open conflict over vital resources such as water wells and pasturage. In addition the family dealt with problems of infertility in almost every marriage. Sarah, Rebekah, and Rachel all struggled to keep the family alive by bearing children. And severe famine chased the family on more than one occasion. In fact, it was just such a famine during the days of Joseph that drove the whole family to Egypt, an Egypt that offered Israel food, land, and work—rescue from certain death.

But the family had never faced anything like this dilemma. What had begun as their salvation now looked to be their demise. Generations of hyper-population growth coupled with a new dynasty on the throne of Egypt wrote Israel's death warrant. The new Pharaoh was terrified of his imagination; Israel might rise up in rebellion or join a foreign invader to overthrow Egypt and take over. And regardless of whether his fear was realistic or merely perceived, it leads to drastic consequences for Israel.

At first the Pharaoh increased the Israelites' workload to deadly levels in order to demoralize them and stop their population growth (Exodus 1:9-14). When this strategy backfired, and the oppressed produced even more children, the Pharaoh instituted a secret plan to kill Israel's male babies at birth; a more dominant female slave population would be easier to control, so he thinks. But the midwives thwart his plan; they respect the Lord more than they respect Pharaoh and will not kill the boys (Exodus 1:17-21). So Pharaoh introduces his "final solution" to the Israelite problem. No more indirect or secret schemes. Now all Egypt is recruited to find and dispose of all Israelite male infants. Expose them, toss them into the river, and be done with the threat to Egyptian security (Exodus 1:22). No, Israel had never faced anything like this crisis.

Earlier in his life Moses had seen a holocaust. He himself was a survivor, thanks to a calculating mother, a faithful sister, and a compassionate member of the royal household. His mother had obeyed Pharaoh's orders to the letter; she put Moses in the river—but she also put a small "ark" between him and the water and then set him in just the right place for Pharaoh's daughter to find him. After all, a daughter of Pharaoh is unlikely to bathe at just any place or time in the river. So, the women combine to save Moses' life and his future; he neither dies nor becomes an Israelite slave.

The young Moses knows his true identity, recognizes the crisis, and even tries to intervene, to make a difference by stopping one instance of abusive Egyptian behavior, a slave master beating an Israelite slave (Exodus 2:11-12). But his efforts blow up in his face. He had killed the slave master in secret, so he thought. But by the next day word is out all over Egypt. The Israelites show no appreciation and the Pharaoh cannot tolerate such subversion of the system. Moses had to run into the wilderness for his own life.

He had seen the problems, tried to help, and failed. But that was forty years past, a lifetime ago and a distant world. Now, he is in the middle of nowhere, far removed from society and from the problems back in Egypt. He is doing nothing special beyond raising a family and tending his own business, trying to keep a bunch of dumb sheep from hurting or killing themselves. Life is not so bad; it is settled and relatively safe and secure. Moses has no grand ambitions for his life, no ambitions at all—when God summons Moses' attention.

A burning bush that just keeps on burning tends to attract a person's attention. It certainly does for Moses. His first words recorded in Scripture are "I must turn aside and look at this great sight, and see why the bush is not burned up" (3:3). His curiosity demands an investigation; God has his attention and as Moses comes near the bush God begins His introductory words. First, God calls Moses by name (3:4), another startling development. Whoever or whatever is responsible for the bush that keeps on burning already knows Moses by name. Second, the voice demands immediate removal of footwear. This is holy ground! Do not walk on holy ground like it is a common desert path. Third, this "God-in-a-bush" offers a formal introduction: "I am the God of your father, the God of Abraham, the God of Isaac, and the God of Jacob" (4:6a).

Moses first approached the bush out of his own curiosity. He had to see what this was all about. By the time God finishes His introductory words Moses is barefooted, scared out of his wits, and hiding his face. This flame is no natural desert phenomenon; this is his family's God, a God who knows him by name, summoning his attention.

With Moses' attention secured beyond distraction the Lord begins to explain:

> I have observed the misery of my people who are in Egypt;
> I have heard their cry on account of their taskmasters.
> Indeed, I know their sufferings, and I have come down to
> deliver them from the Egyptians, and to bring them up out of
> that land to a good and broad land, a land flowing with milk

and honey, to the country of the Canaanites, the Hittites, the Amorites, the Perizzites, the Hivites, and the Jebusites. The cry of the Israelites has now come to me; I have also seen how the Egyptians oppress them. (3:7-9)

This announcement has to be the best of news to Moses! The God of Israel has heard the Israelite cry, has come down to bring them out of oppression and to bring them into the fertile land of promise. Praise God! This God-in-a-bush might be a bit hard of hearing; Moses heard this cry forty years ago. He might be a bit slow to act; Moses had already tried to do something himself. But at least, at last, the God of Israel declares that He is aware and is going to deal decisively with the situation. This good news is worth the hike up a mountainside to hear.

But the Lord is not finished with His speech: "So come, I will send you to Pharaoh to bring my people, the Israelites, out of Egypt" (3:10). Life has a way of turning on a few small words. "Come," God says, "I will send you," and while I can only imagine Moses' thoughts, I think we can get close to what raced through his mind at that moment. Where did that come from? Wait just a minute, God-in-a-bush—what happened to all your statements that "*I* have heard," "*I* have come down to deliver," and "*I* will bring them up"? Go for it, God. Get on down to Egypt and rescue your people. Send plagues, work miracles. Maybe you should even lead them out to the Sea of Reeds and then divide it so they can walk across on dry ground; that would make a great movie! Take your people to the land of promise and have them conquer it with crazy military strategies like walking around a city for seven days, shouting, and the city walls falling flat. Do whatever you need to do, but what in the world does any of this have to do with me?

God's commission to Moses is not ambiguous or hard to understand. It's just crazy, the most preposterous thing Moses has ever heard in his life. If the God of Israel wants to deliver His people out of Egypt then He should just do it, Moses objects. But leave me out of this; I am nobody. I have neither the power, the resources, the status, nor the desire to think about doing such a thing. Pharaoh is not going to just let me waltz into Egypt and take these people out. Maybe this God-in-a-bush has been in the sun too long or the smoke has gone to His head; I am in no way the right person for this job (3:11). But God is not offended, flustered, or concerned with Moses' hesitancy, at least not yet. As we have seen in our study of the call narratives, these events typically include an objection from the one called. Moses' objection, then, is no more unusual or unexpected than an attorney cross-examining a witness. In fact, a servant who does not raise an objection to his or her calling may not adequately understand the call or the stakes involved. We expect to hear an objection in this situation and Moses does not let us down.

God does not reprimand Moses for stating the obvious problem. But God also does not respond the way we might anticipate. God reassures Moses, according to the pattern, but He does not overturn or correct Moses' assessment of the situation. The Lord does not tell him that he can do this, that he has the necessary talent, charisma, or status. The Lord does not build up Moses' ego or self-confidence. Instead, God says, "I will be with you" (3:12) and follows the script of a call narrative perfectly by offering Moses a sign of divine favor: When you have brought the people out of Egypt, you will worship God on this same mountain, and then you will know that I sent you and have been with you (3:12). The only catch is that the sign is set in the future rather than the present. Only after Moses has carried out the first half of his commission (bringing the people out of Egypt) will the sign verify God's presence with him. Nonetheless, at least it is something to hold on to.

According to the way things are supposed to happen in a call narrative, Moses should now pack for a trip to Egypt. We have seen a

crisis looming in Egypt, a summons to attention in the burning
bush, and introductory words from God about His concern for
Israel with stress on His relationship to Moses. God has commissioned Moses with a clear and specific task, Moses has raised his
objection, and the Master has reassured His servant of His presence
and offered a sign of divine favor. The call is supposed to be over.
The groom has kissed the bride and the minister has presented the
newly married couple to the audience. All that is left to do is to leave.

But Moses does not move. God's reassuring words to his first
objection only lead to another objection. Loosely paraphrased
Moses asks, "That's wonderful that **you** will be with me, but **who are
you**? If I show up in Egypt what am I to say when they ask what God
sent me?" Moses again seems to raise a reasonable objection, even if
it does begin to push the limits of what should be happening here.
He asks: Who are you? What is your name? And his request probes
beyond a mere name for critical information about the adequacy of
this God. Are you simply a God-in-a-bush with great ideas but little
power? How do you rate among the Egyptian pantheon of gods of
my youth? What can you do besides set a bush on fire? If you are
who you claim to be, why now? **Who are you?**

The Lord's response to Moses' question merits extensive discussion that must be deferred to others. For our purposes two observations must suffice. First, God does provide Moses with His name:
"Thus you shall say to the Israelites, 'The LORD, the God of your
ancestors, the God of Abraham, the God of Isaac, and the God of
Jacob, has sent me to you': this is my name forever, and this my title
for all generations" (3:15). God supplies Moses with a name, trans-
lated here as "LORD" (from the Hebrew *yhwh*) with small case capital letters to distinguish this name from the word "lord" (from the
Hebrew *'dwn* meaning "master or sovereign"). Second, as is typical
for words of reassurance in a call narrative, God reiterates the original commission and reassures Moses that despite certain difficulties

he will be successful because of the Lord's support. Moses will go to Egypt and tell the Israelite leaders that the Lord has sent him to bring them up out of Egypt to the land of promise (3:16-17). Pharaoh, however, is not going to let the people walk out without a fight (3:18-19). But the Lord will force him by striking Egypt with wonders (plagues) so that the Israelites will not only leave Egypt, they will plunder the Egyptians when they leave (3:20-22).

God's call to Moses is now doubly completed. Twice the minister has pronounced the bride and groom to be husband and wife and twice the couple has kissed. Moses has objected twice and twice the Lord has responded with reassuring words and a restatement of his commission. Now Moses should exit for Egypt with God escorting him; but he still does not move. He still does not accept his calling.

This refusal is not the way it is supposed to happen. Moses' first and second objections ("Who am I?" and "What do I say is your name?") lead to a third: What if they do not believe me when I say the Lord appeared to me (4:1)? Again, I take this objection to be reasonable, but also revealing. Why would Israelites suffering Egyptian oppression all these years believe that the Lord appeared to Moses in the wilderness? They might want to believe it, but a God-in-a-bush speaking to an outcast in the wilderness and then sending this one man to deliver them from the mighty Egyptian empire pushes the limits of credibility. Why indeed? The Lord also appears to accept the reasonableness of Moses' third objection. Rather than rebuke, the Lord offers three more signs (in addition to the sign from 3:12): the staff-to-snake-to-staff sign (4:2-5), the hand-to-leprous-to-clean sign (4:6-7), and the water-to-blood sign (4:9). God assures Moses, they will believe that He, the God of their ancestors, has appeared to him and sent him with this task.

We may have already detected from the first two objections the underlying reason why Moses continues to object rather than accept God's call, but his third objection makes it fairly hard to miss. Moses thinks this call is about Moses. His objections all focus on a single theme: himself. Who am *I*? What will *I* say? What if they do not believe *me*? To which God consistently tries to get Moses to see beyond himself. *I* (God) will be with you. *I* am the Lord, the God of your ancestors. *I* will work through you in such a way as to bring success (3:18-22). They will believe *I* sent you (4:2-9). Moses, God says, your call is not about you, your abilities, your knowledge, or your credibility; your call is about me, the Lord. But Moses cannot see it.

> **For a man who claims not to speak well, [Moses] is certainly good at arguing with the Lord.**

Moses objects for a fourth time, again about himself: "Oh my Lord, I have never been eloquent, neither in the past nor even now that you have spoken to your servant; but I am slow of speech and slow of tongue" (4:10). Perhaps Moses is correct; maybe he is not an able orator or has some physical speech disability. Perhaps. But I get the sense that Moses is pushing his luck. For a man who claims not to speak well, he is certainly good at arguing with the Lord. If he is able to argue with Pharaoh half as well as he is arguing with God, getting Israel out of Egypt is going to be a walk in the park.

This time the Lord's response cuts to the core issue. Moses, you are still missing the point. This call is not about you, your power, your credibility, or your ability to speak well. Do you think I do not know your abilities and limitations? Who do you think made you? Who made your mouth? The issue is not what you feel capable of doing; I decide who is capable or not. The point is that I will be with you and supply the necessary ability for success (4:11-12). To accept his call Moses must recognize a simple fact: this is not his call, but God's call and it is not about Moses, it's about God.

Moses tries one more time to get God to see it his way: "O my Lord, please send someone else" (4:13). Finally, he has run out of reasonable objections and states what has been the real excuse all along: *I do not want to do this.* Despite the Lord's reassurances and correctives, Moses still thinks this is about Moses—his lack of power, his inability, his flawed talent, and most of all—his lack of desire. He just does not want to go, to upend his life just for this God-in-a-bush and his crazy plan. So now, the Lord's reassuring words take a decidedly different path. God is frustrated and angry (4:14a) and offers Aaron to Moses as an assistant (4:14b-16), a concession not necessarily in God's original plan. But in the final assessment the Lord tells Moses, "Take in your hand this staff, with which you shall perform the signs" (4:17) and reading what seems obvious between these lines: AND GO!

Just as we saw with Abraham and Sarah, the issue in this story is not discerning God's voice or understanding God's call. If God needs to light a bush to get a person's attention, God can light a bush; God's servants need not go wandering in the wilderness searching for the voice of God. Further, Moses' bush comes with caller I.D. and a crystal clear signal. Moses knows who is calling and he knows what God is calling him to do; he just doesn't want to do it. Perhaps he thinks that life is nicely settled; *I have a decent job and a young family.* Maybe he recalls his earlier failure; *I thought you had called me then, I tried to help, and it landed me out here.* Certainly Moses thinks that he is not the right man for this job; *I have neither the talent, status, nor power to do such a thing.* But regardless of what Moses might be thinking, in the final analysis Moses is considering only one thing: Moses.

The self-absorption of our culture pushes us to the same conclusion. Discerning God's will is not our problem, not really. Our struggle is that we are tempted to think that if God calls us, the call must be about us, our needs, our concerns, our abilities. God's call to Moses reminds us that it is not. And God's call to Moses reminds us that our excuses fall as flat and often sound just as self absorbed as his. We couldn't possibly do that (but I am with you). We don't have the talent, financial resources, or power to do such a thing (but I am with you). That's too outrageous, too risky (but I am with you). We tried that before and it failed, just caused more problems (but I am with you). Some people are not going to like this (but they are not the ones who call you, I am with you). Lord, please...

God's call has never been about the one called, but about the One who calls...

But the Lord explains to Moses (and us) that His call upon our lives is not about us, our ability, our resources, our desires, or our personal fulfillment. God's call has never been about the one called but about the One who calls, about God's needs and plans for this world. Our call is to surrender ourselves to this audacious, risk-taking God.

Discussion Questions:

1. Read Exodus 2. In what ways did God prepare Moses for his future call?

2. Moses failed the first time he tried to help his people. How do you think this initial failure impacted his response to God's call? How do you think it impacted his later leadership of Israel?

3. Read the report from Moses' initial work in Egypt in Exodus 5:1-6:13. Does Moses' work begin well? What happens? How does Moses feel about God's call at the end of chapter 5? How does he feel at the end of 6:13?

4. Where does Moses "cross the line" with his objections? At what point does expected, reasonable objection turn to excuse making? At what point does God begin to get angry or frustrated with Moses?

5. Why do you think Moses believes God's call is about himself? How are our struggles today the same or different? Explain your response.

6. Reflect on a recent discussion at church that debated whether or not to begin a new work or ministry. What objections were raised? Analyze the objections. In what ways were they like or unlike Moses' objections? What can we learn from how Moses handled the situation? About God's provision for us in such circumstances?

chapter 5

Joshua: Call Forwarding
Joshua 1:1-9

Riley was my youth minister during my last years of high school. Single, fresh out of college, I thought him to be an incredibly old and mature twenty-two years old. For some reason he took me everywhere with him: Abilene Bible Teacher's Workshop, Tulsa Soul Winning Workshop, Central Texas Youth Camp, mission trips, seminars, bookstores. I stayed in his room on many of these trips; sometimes he even paid my way so I could go. When I was sixteen, Riley convinced the elders to allow me to preach the Sunday night sermon, my first—twenty five minutes long, seven major points with at least three sub-points each. On occasion, I jogged at night with Riley, not for exercise (he was rather big; I could jog backwards and keep pace) but because back at the cars we would sit and talk. We looked at the stars (he had taken an astronomy class in college and so I considered him something of an expert in this field too) and marveled that the light from some of these stars began its journey when Jesus walked on the earth.

Then there was Brother Cooper and one of those Saturday morning all-church workdays with tasks ranging from spring cleaning around the building, to stuffing envelopes, to making visits. My plan that day was to help clean out the buses or do some painting, maybe even help with the big mail out, anything but join the visitation teams. But Riley had other plans; he assigned me to Brother Cooper as my visitation partner. Now, I was only seventeen and Brother Cooper was old (somewhere between fifty and a hundred in my thinking), bald, and not exactly a teenager's first choice of buddies. He wasn't an elder or even a deacon, so far as I can remember; just one of those older men you always saw at church. Worse, we drew the name of a man who was a member at the church, but who hadn't attended in months. Old man and kid, off to retrieve one of the Lord's lost sheep.

I knew the address, drove by the house all the time; it was just about two blocks up the street that we had just turned on. And then, without warning Brother Cooper took a hard right turn, hit the brakes and turned off the engine. There we sat, Paul and Timothy parked on the side of a city street on a Saturday morning. But before I had a chance to make a run for it, Brother Cooper turned to me and said, "Son, you need to always remember the power of prayer in everything you do." And right there, with cars passing by, Brother Cooper led us in prayer.

I couldn't tell you what he prayed that morning or whether God answered his prayer. I just know that God answered my prayers. When we got the truck running again, and up to the correct address, no one was home.

What was that person's name, the one no one else really noticed but whose quiet presence, simple words, and actions made the difference in your life? Perhaps they saw something in us that no one else could see, or maybe they just had greater imagination for what God could do with an ordinary lump of clay. Whatever the reason, they invested themselves in us. They took the time to encourage uncoordinated, flailing first efforts; they always had the time to listen. They taught us, mentored us, changed us—and most often had no idea the impact they were making on our lives. I had many—Riley, Brother Cooper, my grandfather, just to mention a few. And Joshua had Moses.

Near the end of his life Joshua gathered the leaders of Israel to Shechem and reminded them of the marvelous things God had done from the call of Abram and Sarai to their settlement of the Promised Land. Then he made one last challenge:

> Now therefore revere the Lord, and serve him in sincerity and in faithfulness; put away the gods that your ancestors served beyond the River and in Egypt, and serve the Lord. Now if you are unwilling to serve the Lord, choose this day whom you will serve, whether the gods your ancestors served in the region beyond the River or the gods of the Amorites in whose land you are living; but as for me and my household, we will serve the Lord. (Joshua 24:14-15)

Joshua, one of the most successful leaders of God's people, had made his decision on this subject long before this final scene, a decision documented by his record of service.

Joshua's first task after God called him to replace Moses was to remind some of the family groups of a bargain they had struck with Moses (Numbers 32). The tribes of Reuben, Gad, and half of Manasseh had requested that their people be allowed to settle on the east side of the Jordan. Initially, Moses went ballistic at their proposal; they were repeating their ancestors' failure to conquer the land, faithlessly running from battle again. They assured Moses that they were not skipping out; they would help Israel conquer the western land but they wanted to take their allotment on the east. Moses agreed on these conditions and the matter was resolved. But that was then; that was with Moses and he is not around anymore. Joshua's first task is to ensure that these families keep their promise, and he does it. He confronts the issue head-on and resolves it; the eastern tribes affirm their past agreement (Joshua 1:12-18). And while hardly an ideal first day on the job, this affair was easy compared to what follows.

The next task for this newly-called leader is to get Israel across the Jordan River. The Lord gives Joshua the plan: "have the priests carry the ark down to the river. When their feet hit the water I'll pull back the river so that the people can walk across on dry ground just like at the Sea of Reeds. Joshua, tell the people what is going to happen before you do all this. Tell them first so that they will know that I am with you" (Joshua 3:1-13, paraphrased). I can imagine my response: Lord, wouldn't it make better sense not to say anything until after this is over? After all, announcing such a grand plan doesn't give a leader much of a way out if this does not work. But Joshua doesn't hesitate at all.

Nor does he back down when the Lord gives him his next task. No sooner do they get across the river than the Lord tells Joshua, "Make flint knives and circumcise the Israelites a second time" (Joshua 5:2). The new generation of males, born since the exodus, had not been circumcised (5:4-5) and now, Joshua must convince them—all of them at one time—to do it. Let's admit it, we typically think that God's call is about glamorous, heroic tasks of service that people will admire, not this. And yet Joshua does it with such success that they name the place Gibeah-haaraloth—"the hill of the foreskins" (5:6), an image not likely to be found in an illustrated Bible.

But it's not over. The first battle lies ahead and God has even more unusual plans: "Have the warriors and priests march around Jericho once a day for six days. Then, on the seventh day have them march around the city seven times. When they make a final long horn blast have all the people shout, the city wall will fall flat, and you can storm the city. Joshua, tell the army, priests, people—everyone—this is what you are going to do" (6:2-5, paraphrased). What army in their right mind would do this? This is an order of worship for a religious parade, not a military strategy! This "battle plan" takes away Israel's military advantage as the superior force and places the battle in the hands of God. Exactly–that's the point. And for Joshua this is doubly risky. If this doesn't work he will look like a fool and probably be looking for a new call.

"When God calls" is glamorous only in theory, only in the sermons of the untested, not in practice. Who really wants a call like this? Who seeks out a call that demands risky leadership, confronting touchy issues without flinching, and carrying out battle plans that have only a prayer for success? More, where does someone who is willing to accept such a call come from? People like this do not appear like a magic rabbit out of a hat.

Back to Joshua, back to the very beginning of his story. Joshua's first appearance in the Bible comes as Israel travels across the wilderness toward God's mountain.

> **"When God calls" is glamorous only in theory, only in the sermons of the untested, not in practice.**

Unexpectedly, the Amalekites attack and Moses calls upon Joshua to select an army and lead them into battle the next morning (Exodus 17:8-9). As for Moses, he will stand at a safe distance on top of a hill with Aaron and Hur. Personally, I would prefer any of their assignments to Joshua's; but Joshua does what Moses asks of him. He leads the troops while Moses appeals to God for victory with outstretched hands (see Psalm 28:2; 88:9; 143:6).

Soon Joshua becomes a regular feature of the story, appearing as the "young assistant" (NRSV) or "young aide" (NIV) to Moses. When Moses hikes up the mountain, his "assistant Joshua" goes with him (Exodus 24:13); when Moses comes back down, so does Joshua (Exodus 32:15,17). Moses pitches a tent for God outside the camp and "his young assistant" stays there (Exodus 33:11). Find Moses in the story and then look around, somewhere nearby will be the young Joshua. Most likely he will not be doing anything partic-

ularly noteworthy. In fact, sometimes his youthfulness and enthusiasm cause him to speak a bit foolishly. Once, on their way down
from the mountain Joshua heard noise from the camp and declared
to Moses that it sounded like war (Exodus 32:17). Moses knew better. Another time, after Moses had complained sharply to the Lord
that he could not handle all his responsibilities, the Lord moved to
appoint seventy leaders to help carry the burden. In order to publicly confirm their new office God caused them to prophesy
(Numbers 11:25). Two of the appointees, however, had not come to
the tent as instructed. And to Joshua's dismay these two prophesied
in the camp! Unacceptable and dangerous, Joshua urged Moses,
"My lord Moses, stop them!" (Numbers 11:28). Moses calms
Joshua's anxiety: "Are you jealous for my sake? Would that all the
Lord's people were prophets, and the Lord would put his spirit on
them!" (Numbers 11:29). Moses sounds a bit like Jesus correcting
the disciple's fierce but misguided enthusiasm; "Master, we saw
someone casting out demons in your name, and we tried to stop
him, because he does not follow with us" (Luke 9:49). I suppose
such comes with the package of taking on a young apprentice. They
will not always get it right.

Prior to the death of Moses, Joshua's most famous role was as
one of the twelve spies appointed by the tribes to explore the land
and bring a report (Numbers 13-14). The report, of course, was
glowing: It is a great land, flowing with milk and honey (Numbers
13:27). But the counsel was dismal. We cannot possibly take the
land—people live there and they have fortified cities! One wonders
what they expected to find: a billboard ("Welcome to Canaan, a
great place to conquer"), a welcome mat, a "For Sale" sign?

Joshua and Caleb challenge the consensus. "If the Lord is pleased
with us, he will bring us into this land and give it to us... do not rebel
against the Lord; and do not fear the people of the land, for they are
no more than bread for us; their protection is removed from them;

and the Lord is with us; do not fear them" (Numbers 14:8-9). And for advocating faith rather than fear, the people threaten to stone them to death (14:10).

In time it becomes clear that Moses will not complete his commission. His own failure to trust will prevent him from taking the people into the land (Numbers 20:9-13), and he will die east of the Jordan, outside the promise. As the Lord summons him to climb the Abraim mountain range to see the land that he will never enter and then to die, Moses raises an important concern: The Lord needs to appoint a new leader, someone who will complete the task. God can't leave Israel like sheep without a shepherd (Numbers 27:12-17). Without hesitation God responds, take Joshua, commission him before all Israel, lay your hands on him and give him authority to lead (27:18-23). Isn't the solution obvious, Moses? Hasn't it been obvious for a long time?

Moses does as God instructs and from this point on, it seems that Moses is even more deliberate in his mentoring and encouraging of his "young aide." He tells Joshua,

> Be strong and bold, for you are the one who will go with this people into the land that the Lord has sworn to their ancestors to give them; and you will put them in possession of it. It is the Lord who goes before you. He will be with you; he will not fail you or forsake you. Do not fear or be dismayed. (Deuteronomy 31:7-8)

So, after a long, circuitous route, we finally come to Joshua's call narrative (Joshua 1:1-9). And after all this, his call seems a bit anti-climactic. There is a looming crisis with the death of Moses and the people still outside the land, but nothing much is made of it in the text. Nor is there anything special about the summons to attention, except that it is nearly non-existent. God simply begins to speak to

Joshua, and unlike Abraham or Moses, there is no hint that this call is disruptive to Joshua's plans or unexpected in the least.

The introductory word is equally underwhelming, only five words in English (three in Hebrew): "My servant Moses is dead" (Joshua 1:2). It seems a bit of an odd thing to tell Joshua; doesn't he already know that Moses is dead? Perhaps not—after all, Moses went up the mountain, died, and was buried in an unmarked grave (Deuteronomy 34:5-6). But I suspect Joshua already knew. God is not telling him new information but making sure Joshua understands what this information means for him. Moses is dead. Do you understand? It's your turn.

God's commission is as obvious as it is daunting: take the people and proceed across the Jordan into the land I am giving to them (1:2). Of all the calls in Scripture, this is the one we could have predicted. Sure, lead the people into the promised land, finish the task God put before Moses. But our foresight in no way diminishes the astounding stress of the call: Take *these people*, *these people* who bucked God and Moses since Egypt, *these people* who complain at the drop of manna, *these people* who still think returning to Egypt is a valid option. Joshua knows *these people* and knows that dealing with the Canaanite resistance will be the easiest part of his call, the harder part will be dealing with *these people*!

And yet, we do not hear a single word of objection from Joshua. The next thing we know Joshua commands the people to get ready to cross the Jordan (1:10-11). To be sure, God still offers reassurance. The Lord tells Joshua that He is not only giving the land to Israel, it is as good as "given" (1:3). No one will be able to withstand Joshua (1:5). Just as the Lord was with Moses, so He will be with Joshua (1:5,9). God reiterates the commission (1:6) and urges Joshua to "be strong and courageous" (1:6), "only be strong and very courageous" (1:7), "be strong and courageous; do not be frightened or dismayed, for the Lord your God is with you wherever you go" (1:9). The idea is emphatic, but easily mistaken. God is not urging Joshua to find his inner reserves, to strengthen himself. No, the Lord reminds Joshua to find strength in the Lord. The psalmist uses the same battle language and writes, "Wait for the Lord; be strong, and let your heart take courage; wait for the Lord!" (Psalm 27:14; see also 31:24).

No question about it, Joshua 1:1-9 is a call narrative, and yet other than God's reassurances it is hardly remarkable. The summons to attention is not disruptive or unexpected. There is little in the way of an introductory or explanatory word, and the one called does not offer a single objection. Joshua's call is exceptional only because it is so unremarkable—and yet, it is obvious why. Moses has been preparing Joshua for this moment for the past forty years and Joshua has been preparing himself for this call all of his life. So as a result, this call is not surprising, needs little introduction, no explanation, and receives no objection. We all saw it coming miles before we got to the Jordan river.

Joshua did not become the next great leader of Israel by sitting alone in his tent trying to figure out God's call on his life, and Moses did not prepare the next leader for God's call by accident. Joshua faithfully did whatever the community, Moses, or God needed him to do: lead an army, follow Moses up and down the mountain, stay behind at the tent, or spy out the land. God put him where God wanted him and his task was to do what was set before him, not search for some greater call. Once again, discerning God's call is not the called person's responsibility; it was not Joshua's worry, nor should it be ours. Instead, Joshua's focus was on doing what he needed to do in the present moment and place. God (and Moses) took care of the rest.

It is also hard to miss the role that Moses, himself called by God, played in the call of Joshua. Moses must have seen or at least imagined something for the young man, some talent, some future. So he began Joshua's training, purposely grooming him for the day he would no longer be around to lead Israel. Joshua's presence on the mountain, at the tent, everywhere we see Moses is no accident—Moses mentors this "young servant." At times Joshua sounds as inept as Peter: It sounds like war, Moses. Make them stop prophesying, Moses. But Moses sticks with him. And when, especially when, Joshua's future becomes clear to Moses, he becomes more deliberate in his instruction and encouragement. God may call Joshua, but Moses got him ready.

Joshua's call, then, leaves us with two questions from two different perspectives: One, are we being faithful to the tasks God and our own community of faith set before us? Are we preparing ourselves for future calls by our faithfulness to present needs? Two, who are we getting ready for God's call? Who can we imagine picking up our own roles and tasks for the next generation? Both questions demand conscious decisions: mentoring is a lot of trouble (it would be easier to go solo) and faithfulness in the present is more difficult than dreaming of what God might call me to do in the future. We need both sides of this equation. We need more Joshuas ready to serve in the mundane as needed, and we need more Brother Coopers—no official leader, but a faithful man willing to take a kid along for the ride.

Discussion Questions:

1. What do you think was Joshua's single greatest act of leadership? Explain.

2. How do you imagine the people responded to Joshua's unusual or radical requests (e.g., crossing the river on dry ground, marching around Jericho, circumcision)? How do you think Joshua handled these concerns? What response do you think you might have had to Joshua?

3. After the death of Joshua (Joshua 24:29-31; Judges 2:6-10) no single great leader emerged in Israel. What do you make of this development? Was this inevitable with the dispersion of the tribes in the territory or do you think it indicates a failure? Explain.

4. Name the people through whom God has especially worked in your life. Share the stories of how they specifically helped you. What did they do to encourage and challenge you?

5. What are your roles of service and leadership? When you were younger did you ever imagine yourself being in these roles? What brought you to this point?

6. Who are the younger people in your life like Joshua? Who are you mentoring for roles of service and leadership? What can you do now to prepare them for their life in ministry? Conclude your study time with prayer for these young people and for your service to them.

chapter 6

Jacob: Let's Make a Deal

Genesis 28:10-22

We have seen that "calling" in ancient Israel happened in a predictable fashion much like our own weddings, funerals, graduations, and other important life events. We have also seen that when God called people in the Old Testament He often used a common form. The people were familiar with this way of calling and through it they could make sense of their own encounter with the divine as well as explain it in understandable terms to those around them. With a crisis looming in the background, a master would summon the attention of a servant from his or her daily routine. After a few introductory words about the situation or their existing relationship, he would commission the servant to a specific task and endow him with any necessary authority to complete it. Any commission that required a call also warranted an objection from the servant; if not, anybody could do it and why bother with a call? So, the master expected the servant to raise the obvious difficulties to which he responded with reassurance and a reiteration of the commission. Finally, the now duly called servant would go about the master's business. This is just the way calls happened, or at least were supposed to happen. Then there was Jacob.

Jacob's parents were the poster couple on how to raise a dysfunctional family. Dad, Isaac, loves his firstborn, he-man son Esau, the tough hairy hunter who likes the outdoors. Mom, Rebekah, dotes on Esau's younger twin Jacob, Esau's opposite who was a "quiet man, living in tents" (Genesis 25:27), a momma's boy. So, naturally, mom and dad play favorites and aggravate the rivalry between the boys that began, according to the story, even before their birth (Genesis 25:22).

Esau comes across in the story as the ignorant dupe who is too dense to realize that his brother is out to get him and take his role as the firstborn son of the family. On one occasion Esau came home from the field ravenously hungry, about to "starve to death" he thinks. And he falls for it. Jacob offers him food, but only at the price of his birthright, his right to the lion's share of the inheritance and place as the next family patriarch. And Esau does it. He thinks he's going to drop dead unless he gets the food and what good is a birthright if you're too dead to enjoy it? Now, in fairness to Esau, it is possible that he is sharper than he appears. He may think that the birthright is worthless without his dad's blessing on the firstborn—and he knows Isaac would never go for blessing Jacob. He is dad's favorite; his status is beyond Jacob's reach. But Esau wildly underestimates his brother.

Jacob is a bigger jerk than even his brother can imagine. At birth Jacob grabbed hold of Esau's "heel" in an effort to pull him back so that he could be the first born, thus his name Jacob, "heel grabber." It didn't work, Esau still got out first. But now Jacob has manipulated him to grab the birthright and he is only warming up. In a final stroke of opportunism Jacob makes a play for his father's blessing on the first born—led, coached, and assisted by none other than his mother. What a family!

Jacob's ploy works. He tricks blind and feeble Isaac, hardly challenging prey for a man of Jacob's talents, and gains his blessing.

May God give you of the dew of heaven,
  and of the fatness of the earth,

and plenty of grain and wine.
Let peoples serve you,
 and nations bow down to you.
Be lord over your brothers,
 and may your mother's sons bow down to you.
Cursed be everyone who curses you,
 and blessed be everyone who blesses you! (Genesis 27:28-29)

"Be lord over your brothers"—that's all Jacob ever wanted to hear. That's also all that Esau needed to hear to conclude that Jacob has to die. He comes back too late to stop Isaac's irrevocable blessing, even if it was given to a son who played him for a fool, and all that is left is an anti-blessing:

See, away from the fatness of the earth shall your home be,
 and away from the dew of heaven on high.
By your sword you shall live,
 and you shall serve your brother;
but when you break loose,
 you shall break his yoke from your neck. (Genesis 27:39-40)

That's it, the solution is obvious: "break his yoke from your neck"—break Jacob. Jacob has to die (27:41).

The crisis behind Jacob's call then, is both personal and global. Jacob is on the run for his life; it's hard to be called if you are dead. But more, this opportunist manipulator who stops at nothing to get what he wants—this is the one who now carries God's promises to Abraham and Isaac to bless the world. He is the designated heir and he is a distinguished weasel. We sense before we even start reading his call that there is no way this could go smoothly, the way it is supposed to, and our intuition is correct.

On his way to the protective custody of extended family in Haran, Jacob stops for the night at a cheap motel with a pillow as hard as a rock (Genesis 28:11), blissfully unaware of the call that awaits. After all, who would expect God to call this man? Asleep and defenseless, God catches up to Jacob in a dream: There was a stairway connecting heaven to earth, a portal through which angels were coming and going to do their business. And then the Lord was there, standing beside Jacob. Summons to attention achieved with distinction; everyone, especially Jacob is surprised at this turn of events.

The Lord introduces himself, "I am the Lord, the God of Abraham your father and the God of Isaac" (28:13a) and then offers a bit of explanation: I will give you the land on which you sleep; your descendants will be like dust spread out all over the land and through you and them I will bless the world. I will be with you wherever this journey leads and I will bring you back. I will not leave you until I have done all this in your life (28:13-15, paraphrased).

The promises are familiar to us from the call of Abraham and Sarah: descendants, land, blessing to the world. But here, to this man on this occasion they seem like a bad joke. Jacob is a self-centered man who doesn't have a wife much less many descendants, on the run for his life away from this land, and the thought that God could bless anyone through him is unimaginable. We might wonder if perhaps God dialed a wrong number on this call.

We are also left to wonder what, exactly God is calling Jacob to do? The Lord's speech focuses entirely on who is calling and what God promises to do in Jacob's life. And because the promises are so illogical—why this? why him?—the Lord's speech plows ahead into reassuring words before Jacob can say anything. God's call to Moses was clear enough; fetch the Israelites. God's summons to Abraham was unambiguous; go. But what is God's call to Jacob? What is he supposed to do?

The "call" in this dream is implied (rather than explicit) but nonetheless clear and confirmed by Jacob's reaction. The Lord calls Jacob to make him his God just as He was and is the God of Abraham and Isaac. Allow the Lord to be his God and do all these things in his life; just agree, just say yes. And the next morning, Jacob appears to be on the verge of playing along with this God. He worships, sets up the stone pillow as a pillar and anoints it (28:18). He names the place Bethel, house of God (28:19)—a promising start. But then Dr. Jekyll turns back into Mr. Hyde. Jacob wants to make a deal:

> *If* God will be with me, and will keep me in this way that I go, and will give me bread to eat and clothing to wear, *so that* I come again to my father's house in peace, *then* the Lord shall be my God... and of all that you give me I will surely give one tenth to you. (28:20-22)

Jacob never disappoints.

In response to the most undeserved call, Jacob demands to set the terms: Only if and when you prove yourself to me am I willing to consent, but only then and not before. Check back in with me when you have met my conditions. Unbelievable. Call interrupted.

> **...a lot of people see just as clearly that the Lord wants to be their God, to come into their life in a powerful way....but they freeze.**

I suppose it would be impossible to imagine this scene if it didn't happen all around us on such a regular basis. I don't mean that people are seeing portals with angels ascending and descending. But a lot of people see just as clearly that the Lord wants to be their God, to come into their life in a powerful way to change them, bless them, and work a blessing through them. But they freeze. Maybe it's because we don't feel worthy or maybe because we don't want to change. Perhaps we're just stubborn. But Jacob's response is not so unbelievable, not really. What is unbelievable is how God deals with him—and us.

Jacob travels on to Paddan Aram where he lives for the next twenty years (31:38), meets his equal (Laban) in deceitful manipulation, and as a result two significant things happen in his life. First, he marries not just one wife but two sisters and dutifully carries his parents' dysfunction into his marriages; he plays favorites, loves Rachel and tolerates Leah. And as a result the wives, especially Leah, engage in a baby-bearing contest for their husband's love. Leah thinks, hopes that if she gives Jacob one son and then another, and another, that he will come to love her (29:31-34). Rachel, unable to conceive and falling desperately behind in the baby contest, presents Jacob with her maidservant to produce children on her behalf (30:3; remember Sarah and Hagar?). And when Leah sees it, she does the same with her maidservant to keep her advantage (30:9-12). Finally, Rachel herself becomes pregnant and gives Jacob a son (30:22-24), who of course becomes dad's favorite. It's enough to put a marriage counselor in therapy. But what all this dysfunction produces is a large and growing family in Haran.

Second, Jacob becomes filthy rich. How he does it is not entirely clear, but as we would expect with Jacob, his gain comes largely through trickery at the expense of those closest to him. In this case his father-in-law pays the price (30:25-43), an expense duly noted by Jacob's brothers-in-law who love Jacob like a dog loves fleas.

After twenty years, two wives (plus two concubines), eleven sons, one named daughter, and enormous wealth, Jacob finally wears out his welcome (one only wonders what took so long). When he left twenty years earlier it was because Esau was ready to kill him. Now, in a choice between lesser evils, Jacob senses that he has better odds back in the land with Esau than staying with Laban. So again he runs. But in both cases, Jacob cannot escape his past. Laban and

Esau each confront Jacob to resolve their issues. He tries to run away from Laban without so much as a goodbye, taking his daughters, grandchildren, and wealth he had wrested from him. But Laban tracks him down, confronts him, and pushed by God, establishes a treaty with him (31:19-55). In much the same way, when Esau learns that Jacob is coming back he sets out to meet him and, much to Jacob's surprise, to offer reconciliation (32:1-21; 33:1-17).

The primary relationship, however, that Jacob must resolve upon his return to the land is his relationship with the God who called him. When he was running away the first time, Jacob vowed that **if** the Lord would be with him, provide for him, and bring him back home safely, **then** he would make the Lord his God (28:20-22). The Lord has not forgotten Jacob's bargain. Near the end of his time in Paddan Aram the Lord spoke to him, instructed him to go back home, and said, "I am the God of Bethel, where you anointed a pillar and made a vow to me" (31:13). God remembers the deal. And to be fair, Jacob acknowledges that the Lord has been with him (31:5,42). But now the gig is up; the Lord is bringing him back safely to the land.

In the middle of the night, just outside the homeland, Jacob confronts "a man" and wrestles. It is the story of his life, struggling for an advantage, trying to manipulate the best for himself out of every situation. And once again he prevails, albeit injured, limping and with a new name. His wrestling partner declares him to be Israel, one who struggles with God (32:28), a befitting summary of his entire life. Then suddenly Jacob/Israel realizes he has just had another encounter with the God who called him and to whom he made a vow. He names the wrestling arena Peniel, "face of God" (32:30).

Jacob moves to the city of Shechem and in a promising development, builds an altar that he names El-Elohe-Israel, "God-the God of Israel" (33:18-20). In a subtle naming move, he begins to acknowledge something about his new relationship to the Lord, begins to make good on a twenty-year-old promise. But soon God calls him to go all the way: "Arise, go up to Bethel, and settle there. Make an altar there to the God who appeared to you when you fled from your brother Esau" (35:1). The implication is clear: When you were on the run twenty years ago I called you, asked you to make me your God, and allow me to bless your life and bless others through you. Do you remember Jacob? Do you also recall that you interrupted my call with your list of demands: Only if I was with you, only if I protected and provided for you and brought you back here safely would you make me your God. Jacob, I've done everything you asked. It's time to pay up. "Make an altar to the God who appeared to you"; make me your God.

Jacob does not miss the point. He tells his household to get rid of their gods and purify themselves (35:2). He knows this is about who will be the God of his life; competing gods have to go. The family will move to Bethel so that, Jacob explains, "I may make an altar there to the God who answered me in the day of my distress and has been with me wherever I have gone" (35:3). The Lord has done what I demanded; we are going to Bethel and settle this.

At Bethel the call that Jacob interrupted twenty years prior resumes. The Lord picks up where Jacob stopped him: "I am God Almighty, be fruitful and multiply; a nation and a company of nations shall come from you, and kings shall spring from you. The land that I gave to Abraham and Isaac I will give to you, and I will give the land to your offspring after you" (35:11-12). What do you say this time, Jacob? I've done all that you asked, now will you make me your God?

Again, Jacob worships, sets up a stone pillar and anoints it. He again names the place Bethel, house of God. But this time there are no deals to be made, no bargains to strike. Jacob, it appears, finally accepts God's call on his life.

While Jacob's response to God is hardly surprising, after all he is still "heel-grabber," I find God's actions staggering. God does not react like I would: I offered you a great deal Jacob—land, children, blessing. Not only did you not deserve any of it, I should have done the opposite and brought your treachery down on your pompous head. You treat your family like stray dogs and then you dare resist my call? Who do you think you are? Who are you to demand concessions, negotiate a deal on your terms? Forget you! Who needs you? I don't have to put up with this rubbish. Disconnect the call.

But God doesn't seem flustered at all with Jacob; He doesn't give up as easily as I do. To God, Jacob is worth twenty years of divine waiting to resume a call interrupted. And if good-for-nothing Jacob is worth it, I suspect we are too. And I suspect many of us need that divine patience to make good on calls and promises that we have put off, the things we have always said we would do when we are out of school, when we get into school, when we get married, when we have children, when the children leave home, when we retire, when God meets every condition we have placed on Him... Jacob's call leaves us to answer a simple question: Is it time to make a trip to Bethel?

Discussion Questions:

1. What is your general opinion of Jacob? Is he a man of integrity and character? Do you know people like Jacob?

2. What do you think of Esau's character? Why do you think God calls Jacob instead of Esau? What does this teach us about God?

3. Have you ever, like Jacob, made a deal with God when you found yourself in difficult circumstances? Why did you make it? How did it turn out?

4. In what ways does Jacob's growing up in a dysfunctional family impact his own marriages and children? How common do you think that is today?

5. What is God's call to Jacob? What does God expect or want him to do? Why do you think God was so patient in waiting for Jacob? What do we learn about God in this call narrative?

6. Do you think Jacob ever makes good on his vow to God? On a scale of one to ten, does Jacob ever really change for the better?

7. Describe what God is like in this story. How does God act toward Jacob? Why? Is that what you would expect God to do? Please explain.

chapter 7

Isaiah: Here Am I, Send Me!

Isaiah 6

It was "the year that king Uzziah died" (Isaiah 6:1), a fact that may be no more than a time marker, or may serve to alert the reader to something of a national crisis. Uzziah (Azariah) reigned fifty-two years over Judah (II Kings 15:1-2), longer than any other king including David, and oversaw an era of almost unprecedented military and political success (II Chronicles 26:5-15). He "did what was right in the sight of the Lord" (II Kings 15:3), at least until his pride led him to offer his own incense in the temple and God struck him with leprosy (II Chronicles 26:16-21). And yet, despite this failure and the need for his son Jotham to become co-regent in charge of the palace (II Kings 15:5), the nation continued to prosper under his reign. And then Uzziah died.

Assyria had long been the superpower of the ancient Near East, exercising control over a vast empire that included much of Palestine. North of Judah, about the time of Uzziah's death, there was growing unrest, a frustration with Assyrian domination that was fermenting into an anti-Assyrian coalition of nations. Soon this league of nations would exert pressure on Uzziah's son (Jotham) and grandson (Ahaz) to join them in their rebellion (Isaiah 7:1). Under Uzziah's leadership the nation successfully navigated troubled international waters, but now the king is dead.

The reader of the book of Isaiah, however, realizes an even greater crisis. The people of Judah are in serious trouble with God, a sobering revelation made clear by the preceding five chapters. The nation has lost all spiritual sense (1:3) and forsaken the Lord (1:4). Religious practices have become a farce of true religion. The priests and people conduct all the right ceremonies in all the right ways: sacrifices and incense abound, assemblies meet on schedule, festivals run their course. But God has had enough of this charade. Their lives contradict their clamor. They do not share the Lord's passionate concern for justice and righteousness, much less for the defense of the orphan and widow (1:16-17, 21, 23; 5:7). Their only concern is for themselves, their pleasure (5:11-12), their fortunes (5:8), their self-made security (2:6-8), their status symbols (3:18-23). And who or what they ignore or outright oppress to achieve their interests is of no consequence to them (3:14-15).

The first five chapters of Isaiah warn of terrible disaster coming upon Judah because the Lord can no longer tolerate their arrogance. The day of the Lord is coming, and against many assumptions in Judah it will not be a day of more favor and blessing on God's chosen people, but a day that strikes down their pride (2:9-4:1). These chapters conclude with an ominous threat:

> As the tongue of fire devours the stubble,
>   and as dry grass sinks down in the flame,
> so their root will become rotten,
>   and their blossom go up like dust;
>   for they have rejected the instruction of the Lord of hosts,
>   and have despised the word of the Holy One of Israel.
>
> (5:24)

Isaiah's call comes with this dismal warning as the immediate background.

As Isaiah retells his story, God's call to him comes in three discernable movements. First, Isaiah is overwhelmed by a vision in which he catches just a glimpse of the sovereignty and majesty of the Lord. The king of Judah may be dead, but Isaiah quickly learns that THE KING is still seated on a throne and it is a majestic sight, more than Isaiah can take in or describe. The Lord's throne is high and lofty and the hem of His robe overflows the temple. Seraphs, angelic beings closely associated with the divine in ancient thought, hover about the throne. With six wings each they fly, cover their faces lest they view the divine presence and die, and cover their "feet," most likely a euphemism for sexual organs (e.g., 1 Samuel 24:3). Like the priests of Israel, they dare not expose themselves in God's presence (see Exodus 28:42).

Isaiah observes that in the presence of God these six angelic beings continue a cadence of call and response:

> Holy, holy, holy is the Lord of hosts;
> The whole earth is full of his glory. (6:3)

What else can be said? And as they express the best that human words can say about this King, an earthquake shakes in approval and the temple fills with smoke (6:4). Isaiah dares not say more, certainly he does not engage in the lethal folly of trying to describe the Lord himself. He is overwhelmed by this vision of the King who reigns in absolute holiness, and this sense of awe is where his call begins.

In response to his new awareness of the Lord, in the second movement of his call, Isaiah is overwhelmed by a new sense of his own sinfulness. Once Isaiah sees God, he sees himself as he really is—a dead man. "Woe is me" is the language of death. He is dead and lost because in the presence of the holy God he realizes his own sinfulness: "I am a man of unclean lips" (6:5). Perhaps, in comparison to others Isaiah might be able to conclude otherwise, that he is not so bad and may be even good by comparison. But not now. Once Isaiah catches a glimpse of God he sees the true basis for any comparison and realizes he is done for. And not only does Isaiah recognize this standard for himself, but for his entire generation, for all of Judah and beyond. "I live among a people of unclean lips," he says, "yet my eyes have seen the King, the Lord of hosts" (6:5). This vision of the holy can only mean death.

God's purpose, however, is not to overwhelm Isaiah with guilt. Instead, in classic ancient Near Eastern symbolism, one of the seraphs takes a burning coal from the altar and touches Isaiah's lips with it. On the lips of a man who confesses "unclean lips" the coal purifies not just his mouth, but his entire being. His guilt departs and his sin is blotted out, eradicated from existence (6:7). God has not left him to wallow in guilt, but has given him new life! Isaiah, then, is properly overwhelmed, first by a renewed vision of the sovereignty and holiness of the Lord, then by the immediate realization of his sinfulness in the presence of this God, and finally by the Lord's saving work in his life.

Now the Lord poses an open question to those gathered in the divine court. Someone needs to do something about Judah, but who? Whom should I send? Who would be willing to go on our behalf? (6:8) And before the Lord is able to go any further, before there is any explanation of what this commission will entail, Isaiah becomes the eager student in the front of the classroom with hand held high begging the teacher, "Send me!" (6:8). Hardly able to contain his enthusiasm, Isaiah volunteers without even knowing for what he is volunteering. All he knows is that he has such a fresh understanding of God's sovereign holiness, his own complete sinfulness, and appreciation for God's grace that it doesn't matter what God needs done; he is willing to do it. He knows who is calling and that's enough to accept the commission, whatever it might be.

At this point in the story there is no doubt that God has called Isaiah or that Isaiah has accepted the call, even if what his call entails is not yet clear. It seems to me that many of us have much in common with Isaiah. Like Isaiah we may not have any idea where God's call on our lives will lead. We may have our suspicions, our hopes, or there may be numerous options that God places before us. But if you were to ask what is our calling, we couldn't answer. And that's okay; we can just be like Isaiah. What we do know is something about our God—enthroned, majestic, holy, and we shudder at the thought. What we do realize is our own sinfulness; we have no business in the presence of this God. And most of all we know what this God has done in our lives with a burning coal taken from the altar. This holy Lord has saved us, given us new life.

> Like Isaiah we may not have any idea where God's call on our lives will lead

When we put all this together, just as Isaiah did, it really does not matter "what" God's call may entail, only that we are ready and willing to do whatever God needs done in this world. Nor does it matter to us or Isaiah if God singles us out by name. "Who will go for us" is an open call to anyone who is willing to serve. And so we, with Isaiah, eagerly respond, "Here we are, send us."

But maybe we shouldn't speak so fast. If Isaiah had only waited to find out what his commission would be before he accepted it, he might have run the other way. We might too.

In what is perhaps the most perplexing commission ever given, the Lord tells Isaiah to go and say,

> "Keep listening, but do not comprehend;
>   Keep looking, but do not understand."
> Make the mind of this people dull,
>   and stop their ears,

and shut their eyes,
  so that they may not look with their eyes,
    and listen with their ears,
    and comprehend with their minds,
    and turn and be healed. (6:9-10)

Read it again and again, but no matter how we read it, these instructions just don't seem right. God calls Isaiah to preach in such a way as to dull the people's minds, plug their ears, and put them to sleep. To be honest, this is one call that I think I could actually accomplish as a preacher; I can bore people to sleep. But how can this be God's commission to Isaiah? Preach so that they will not turn and be healed?

There are several ways to approach this interpretive problem. One is to follow the lead of the ancient Greek translation and change the sense of the verbs from commands ("do this") to results ("this is what will happen as a result of your preaching"). The TNIV supplies a footnote with this translation: "'You will be ever hearing, but never understanding; you will be ever seeing, but never perceiving.' This people's heart has become calloused; they hardly hear with their ears, and they have closed their eyes." So, instead of failure being God's desire or intent, it is the expected result of Isaiah's work.

A second resolution to the problem is to read the text as sarcasm. The one way to get a stubborn person to do something they don't want to do is to tell them, plead with them, beg them **not** to do it. Then, maybe they will. Perhaps this is what God intends for Isaiah's ministry. God wants His people to turn back and be healed but knows that the only way they will ever listen is if Isaiah tells them not to listen.

These may be correct readings. Isaiah, however, seems to hear God's commission as it initially appeared to us, a call to further harden the people beyond repentance. He immediately objects,

"How long, O Lord?" (6:11a): an objection that may ask for a time frame, or may be a more fundamental reaction to what he has just heard. In the Psalms, for example, the complaint "how long" is not a request for information but a rhetorical question that expects the answer "it has already been too long" whatever the problem might be. So here, Isaiah's response may denote disbelief that this could be God's will or His commission. How can this be God's call on my life? How am I supposed to do this? How long, O Lord?

The Lord responds to both levels of Isaiah's objection. He reassures Isaiah that he has heard correctly; God intends the near complete destruction of his people. And he tells him how long his ministry is to last.

> Until cities lie waste
> without inhabitant,
> and houses without people,
> and the land is utterly desolate;
> until the Lord sends everyone far away,
> and vast is the emptiness in the midst of the land.
> Even if a tenth part remains in it,
> it will be burned again,
> like a terebinth or an oak
> whose stump remains standing
> when it is felled.
> The holy seed is its stump. (6:11-13)

I can only imagine the thoughts racing through Isaiah's mind now: What was I thinking? Why couldn't I keep my big mouth shut? When I said, "Here am I, send me" this is not what I thought I was signing up for! I thought the Lord's call would be about making a difference, changing lives, bringing people back to God—not this, not a ministry that is doomed and even intended to fail from the beginning. How will I ever be faithful to this calling?

Some will imagine even more of Isaiah's feelings because his call resonates deeply with their own experience. I think of Aggie, a Christian woman who has lived out Sarah and Abraham's call to trust God and be a conduit of God's blessing to all around her. She has been faithful to this call in the face of an abusive husband, divorce, chronic and serious health concerns, and meager resources. Perhaps when she first became a Christian, Aggie might have dreamed what God's call would ask of her but who could have imagined this? And I wonder how anyone could be so faithful?

I think of Amber, a former student who graduated from college, took her degree and moved to rural Honduras to live and work among poverty that I cannot imagine. She put "her life" on hold and besides sacrificing her own financial well-being she has to convince others of the worthiness of her work so that she is able to stay in the field. And her story is being replayed countless times in the lives of missionaries all over the world. These sisters and brothers could read Isaiah's mind because it's their own. And I still wonder how anyone could be faithful to such a call?

Christians often find themselves in Isaiah's sandals. Like Isaiah, our lives have been overwhelmed by an awareness of the sovereignty and holiness of our Lord, overwhelmed by our own sinfulness, and even more overwhelmed by God's saving work in our lives. And in response to all this and God's call for someone to do something in this world, we have declared our commitment even before we knew what that declaration would mean for our lives; perhaps we could never really know. But now we wonder "How long, O Lord?" How are we to be faithful to what you have put before us? How, when it is so hard and so fruitless? How, when God's call seems more a ministry of defeat than victory?

I think Isaiah answers our question in this retelling of his story. Listen again, read it again: I saw the Lord, seated on a throne, high and lofty. Absolute holiness. Then I saw myself for the first time as I really am; a filthy person living among filthy people. But then, oh then, I saw what God did and continues to do in my life, my new life thanks to God! You see, it's what made us say yes to God's call in the first place that enables us to remain faithful now. It's when we lose that vision, that insight, that endurance is no longer possible. What solicited our call is what sustains our call. Can we still see Him, the one on the throne? Can we still hear the seraphs calling out "Holy, holy, holy"? Can we still feel the burning coal that changed our lives? Now, can we hear it again: Whom shall I send, and who will go for us?

Discussion Questions:

1. Read Isaiah 1-5. Identify and describe the crises facing Israel when God called Isaiah.
2. If you had been Isaiah, do you think you would have responded in the same way he did? What would you have thought after you learned of your (Isaiah's) specific commission?
3. How do you read Isaiah 6:9-10? Is this God's literal intent for Isaiah's ministry? Explain.
4. Compare Isaiah's call to John's vision on the island of Patmos (Revelation 4). Review Revelation 1-3 and identify the crises facing the churches to whom John writes (e.g., lethargy, persecution). How does John's vision respond to these problems?
5. Do you agree or disagree with the author's claim that only when we see God do we truly see ourselves? Explain your answer. Give an example.
6. Compare Isaiah's response to his vision of God to contemporary claims of visions. How are they similar or different? What do you make of these claims in view of Isaiah's story?
7. Who do you think of when you think of someone who has responded to God's call and is living out that call under difficult circumstances? What seems to keep them going? Share their stories.

chapter 8

Saul: Stopped Cold

Acts 9:1-30; 22:1-21; 26:1-23; Galatians 1:13-17

It's time to take one step closer. Toss the safety net of a neutral objective study into the dumpster and remind ourselves that we are talking about peoples' lives and events that stop life dead in its tracks: The day I stood in our front yard and watched our house burn (I have special appreciation for Moses' burning bush), the morning that church van flipped over. Life goes on, and may get better. But it's not now. Now it feels like a sucker punch that leaves us on our knees gasping for breath. Life may go on, but it will never be the same. So let's drop the professional interpretive distance that protects us from their angst and enables us to walk away untouched. God's call destabilizes and disorients; it calls for radical change. Why anyone who understands this reality would ever seek a direct call from God is beyond me. In the Bible, no one goes looking for it. No one.

Saul was dead set convinced of his calling, and he was obsessed by it. He was the Grand Inquisitor traveling from one place to another, hauling away members of "the Way," as they called it. He had to stop this damnable heresy about a dead and risen messiah, what utter nonsense. He had to shut down this false doctrine leading God's people away from The Truth. And he was willing to do whatever it took. If it meant roughing up a few folks to bring them to their senses, so be it. If it meant killing one or all of them, so be it.

If it meant throwing them in jail so they had time to consider the error of their ways, then so be it. The stakes were heaven high and as he himself said, "I myself was convinced that I ought to do many things against the name of Jesus" (Acts 26:9).

Saul was on his way to a great career in the establishment: highly educated, respected, connections with all the right people. And on this day he was on his way to Damascus authorized to arrest more heretics and bring them back to Jerusalem, not for trial but for punishment; a trial would be an unnecessary waste of time and tax payer's money. He was on his way—when God stopped him cold.

A blinding light stopped him, an oxymoron; light enables sight, darkness blinds, but not this time. Saul is sucker punched to the ground and hears a voice standing over him: "Saul, why are you doing this to me? Why are you out to get me? Don't you know how bad it hurts to keep kicking your foot into a thorn bush? Why do you want to hurt me and bloody yourself?

"Well, sir," Saul said, "if you will tell me who you are maybe I can explain. Who are you?"

"I am Jesus, the one you are persecuting."

Saul hit the brick wall and it fell on him.

"So what do I do now?" Saul asked.

"Go into town, I'll tell you later."

All these years I have been so confident, so sure that this is what is true and that is false. I built my life on my convictions, a good life. Everything was settled; I knew who was in and out, right and wrong. How could this be happening? What have I done? How could I have been so wrong? Not only have I been on the wrong side, I have been hurting, killing those who were right and more—much more than that, I have been persecuting the one they proclaim, their Lord—my God.

No wonder he was dazed: no sight, no food, no drink for three days. Put it in the category of be careful what you ask for, you might just get it. God's call does not leave a person boasting about visions and their unique relationship to God. No, it leaves Moses scrambling barefoot, Isaiah declaring he is a dead man, and Saul blind as a bat.

On the other side of Damascus the Lord placed another call to Ananias, a member of "the Way." God gets his attention through a vision and a single word, his name:

"Ananias"

"Yes, I'm here Lord."

"I need you to get up and go to a house on Straight street; you know the place, Judas's home. There's a man there, a native of Tarsus by the name of Saul. He's praying at this very moment and has seen a vision of a fellow by the name of Ananias, your name—isn't that a coincidence—come lay hands on him so he can regain his sight. Oh yes, I forgot to mention; I appeared to him the other day, blinded him on the spot. Go, would you? He needs you."

Ananias objected, "But Lord, we have heard about this man. He has terrorized your people in Jerusalem and has come here with authority to arrest all of us who confess Jesus as Lord. Now is a good time to lie low, not go introduce myself like some Walmart greeter. It's a trap. He's taking you in with a charade."

"Go anyway. I've chosen him for a special mission; I'm calling him. I'll show him what his call is all about and what the cost will be. But you go, he's waiting."

And the two calls converge. Ananias went to Saul, laid his hands on him, and said, "Brother Saul, the Lord Jesus who appeared to you on the road has sent me so you can see again and be filled with the Holy Spirit." Stuff like fish scales fell out of his eyes and he could see. Ananias continued, "God has chosen you to know His will, see the Righteous One, and to hear His voice. Now you will be His witness to the world. So don't fool around, get up and be immersed to wash your sins away by calling on his name."

I can't decide who was more courageous that day: Ananias who walks into a death-trap just because God told him to go, or Saul who gets up and dies to everything his life ever stood for. He calls on the one he had been out to destroy and then begins to proclaim "He is the Son of God" (Acts 9:20). Granted, the Lord has to whack one on the head and shove the other out the front door, but they both are willing to die when God calls.

God may have had to destroy his world to get him to listen, to hear the call, but once he heard, it changed him.

Ananias fades from the story, and we are left to imagine how God's call impacted the rest of his life. But not with Saul—he will write letters to young churches he established throughout the Roman Empire, and letter after letter will begin the same: "Paul... called to be an apostle" (Romans 1:1; I Corinthians 1:1) or with some other reference to this event, "Paul an apostle—sent neither by human commission nor from human authorities, but through Jesus Christ" (Galatians 1:1; see also Ephesians 1:1; Colossians 1:1; I Timothy 1:1; II Timothy 1:1; Titus 1:1). He will retell his story twice in Acts (22:1-21; 26:1-23) and once in his letter to Galatia (1:13-17). He lived that event on the road to Damascus every day of his life, how could he not? God may have had to destroy his world to get him to listen, to hear the call, but once he heard, it changed him. And anyone who thinks that's easy has never done it.

In January 2005 I attended the Christian Education Association's 44th annual conference in New Orleans. Some years before I had met David Wray, then the chair of the Bible, Missions, and Ministry Department at Abilene Christian University. In his previous life, he was one of the pioneers in education ministry among churches in the Stone-Campbell movement. He served as the education minister at the Highland church of Christ for over 15 years, beginning his work when most had never heard of such a thing. In time, ACU scooped him up to teach the next generation of ministers, a second career at which he has wildly succeeded. The College of Bible has honored David as its Outstanding Faculty Member once and the University recognized him as the Teacher of the Year in 2005.

So when I had a break in my schedule and saw that I could take in one of his classes at the conference, it was a no-brainer decision to go. He began by abandoning his topic and making a confession. In last year's graduate level Church Administration course at ACU he threw out the syllabus and changed ninety to ninety-five percent of the content—**90-95%**. For those not familiar with the sacred halls of academia let me explain: he just broke the sacred rule of academia! No one teaches a class for fifteen years, gets all the lectures written, the syllabus just right, and then tosses it in the bin to start over. No one, except David Wray.

He explained. His career in ministry had been about building programs, promoting the institution, building up the fortress. (In fairness, anyone who knows David would disagree; his work stretched far beyond these limits, but this is his story.) But now he realized that this ministry is not what God calls us to do or become. Instead of building fortresses that can withstand the onslaughts of the enemy, God calls us to set up missional outposts of the kingdom of heaven. Once he saw this, he explained, it changed everything.

In the early 1800's a father and son also began to realize that what they had always believed and practiced could not square with their new insights into Scripture, an insight that drove Thomas and Alexander to a lifetime of change. To cite but one example, both men had been baptized/sprinkled as infants, a practice that neither questioned for years. As members of the Presbyterian Church this practice was simply the way it was done—what was there to discuss? But in time, however, Alexander began to look again and to reach radical conclusions, first about the method of baptism and then its link to the divine forgiveness of sins.

As early as 1809, when Thomas Campbell presented the *Declaration and Address* to the Christian Association of Washington, the topic of sprinkling infants came up, but unexpectedly. As the story goes, Andrew Munro first pointed out to Thomas that if they followed his plan to do only what the New Testament expressly teaches then they could no longer practice infant baptism/sprinkling; neither Thomas, nor Alexander seemed to take his objection seriously, at least not yet. It was not until three years later that Alexander, prompted by the birth of his first child in 1812, concluded that sprinkling was not a New Testament practice and that instead of sprinkling his infant daughter, he needed to be immersed. And so on June 12, 1812, Alexander, his father Thomas, and six others were baptized by Matthias Luse, a Baptist minister. (See the summary of these events in Leroy Garrett's *The Stone-Campbell Movement* [Joplin: College Press, 1981], pp. 177-180.)

Alexander's first step regarding baptism took him toward an association with Baptist churches, a precarious union that lasted some 17 years (1813-1830); but his second moved him away from this community. A milestone in this change was his debate with W.L. Maccala in 1823, eleven years after his own immersion, where for the first time Alexander argued publicly that baptism is linked to the forgiveness of sins, a departure from Baptist doctrine. But he was not finished; his wrestling with baptism was only symptomatic of a person who understood God's call to re-examine honestly every matter, every doctrine—even those he held with confidence. And to approach each subject with an openness to learn and change, not just to confirm and defend the old ideas.

Human nature is opposite of God's call. We all strive to reach points of certainty, from convictions on the best brand of toothpaste to the best route to church on Sunday morning. Then we can settle into a nice routine and relax. The lecture notes for tomorrow are already written, the sermon outline finished, both years ago. My answer to the question that I know my students will ask tomorrow is memorized from repetition. I no longer have to think. I don't have to read or listen to anyone except to point out to them and everyone else where they are wrong. I don't need to study, especially not any of the new ideas. Truth does not change, so what's the point? Best of all, I do not have to worry about being wrong or needing to change. It's not possible; I need not entertain the thought. My calling has shifted from discoverer to enforcer. I've become Saul.

I believe God calls us to more.

My grandfather, R.G. Hatter, was a preacher at heart and a master carpenter by trade. He was a "located" preacher, as he put it, for three churches over a short span, but spent most of his time building "tents" to support his preaching habit. Granddad began his spiritual journey in what is often dubbed the "anti-churches" because of their opposition (anti) to Sunday schools, multiple communion cups, and cooperative church efforts such as orphan's homes. You could not be more conservative in the Stone-Campbell movement. But over the years Granddad kept his eyes and heart open and changed his mind on a good number of subjects. In time he turned and debated leaders among the "anti-churches" and even wrote a tract or two on the subject.

Don't get me wrong, Granddad Hatter did not become a liberal (unless you belonged to the "anti-churches," funny how that works). When the New International Version first hit the presses in the late 1970's the family bought him a copy for Christmas. I still have the Bible in my study, scrawled by his hand inside the front cover: "This is a **wild** translation." Granddad had his limits.

By the time I left for college Granddad and Meemaw had moved to our hometown to be closer to the family. Once he heard that I had decided to major in Bible every trip home was the same. "Granddad wants to see you, has something he has to talk to you about." And I would go, most of the time.

After a few of these sessions about preaching, preachers, and books, granddad decided he was losing time and started writing letters.

March 16, 1980
Hello Glenn David:

I am glad that I have a grandson who wants to be a Gospel Preacher. I am thankful to the Lord Jesus Christ, and I pray that you will never look back—but will press on toward the mark of the high calling of God which is in Christ Jesus. Your road will not always be easy: There will be some bumps and rough places, so be careful to follow the road map given by the Holy Spirit. The Lord does not expect a perfect life, but he does ask us to live a faithful life...

November 1981
Hello Glenn David:

Since you were here a few days ago, I have been thinking about a long talk with you and now I have decided to put it in writing. You are the only grandson I have who is trying to make a preacher. And having some years of experience I am quite sure that I can help you cut a few corners.

First of all I hope that you will study the Bible to learn what it teaches and not to find out how you can defend what some of our brethren teach. The old negro preacher prayed, "Lord help me to get started right, you know how hard I am to change." Don't even believe what I tell you—till you can see that it is in line with the Bible. We as a people claim to, "Speak where the Bible speaks..." I wish it were true.

—

No man in our age had been able to master all of the Bible... May the Lord bless you in your effort.

Grandpa—R.G.H.

Every young preacher should be so blessed to have an older mentor make clear what our call is about—and what it is not about.

God's call is not about staying the same. Never has been. God's call is about listening and changing—and the destabilization such a called life produces. Now I am not suggesting a post-modern agenda in which we throw everything out—there's no truth and anything goes. But I am asking, when was the last time we changed our minds or our practices about anything of substance and why are we so proud that we haven't so much as wobbled on a minor detail in sixty years? This unbending self-confidence is not God's call. God's call to Saul, Ananias, David Wray, the Campbells, R.G. Hatter—their call and our call is to keep our eyes, ears, and hearts open to God's truth. It is God truth, after all; not our truth. Then we might just discover that we've been going at the wrong enemy; we might discover truth that we had been convinced could never be the Truth. We might actually change and grow to be more like Christ than Saul.

> **God's call is about listening and changing—and the destabilization such a called life produces.**

Discussion Questions:

1. Compare the calls of Saul and Ananias to the pattern of a call narrative (see pp 23-26). Are all the parts present? Which are changed or modified? What do you make of these variations?

2. How do you imagine Ananias's call impacted or changed the rest of his life?

3. Who do you know that, like the Campbells or David Wray, came to a fresh understanding of God's will and changed their lives or ministry? Share their stories. What did they realize? In what ways did they change? What were the good and/or bad consequences?

4. In what ways has your understanding of Scripture changed? How has this changed your life?

5. The author claims that we should not be proud of not having changed our minds on anything of substance for years. On a scale of one to ten, to what degree do you agree or disagree with this claim? Why or why not?

6. What were the greatest challenges for Saul to accept his call? For Ananias? For us?

chapter 9

Jonah: Just Say No

Jonah 1—4

Sometimes realizing what a text is not about is the first step to understanding what it is about, especially when the text has a long, strong history of interpretation. In a sense, we need a little demolition of existing assumptions before we reconstruct a framework more in harmony with the author's message. So, we begin our study of Jonah's call with two common emphases about the book of Jonah that aren't really the book's focus.

The book of Jonah is not about God and fish, whether God can create a fish big enough and tame enough to swallow a person whole and then keep him or her alive under water and inside its stomach for three days. The writer doesn't even give God's big fish so much as a "wow" or "cool." It's a non-issue. The text says that God "provided" (1:17) a fish for Jonah just as God also "hurls" the perfect storm on Jonah's cruise (1:4), "appoints" a bush that in one night grows large enough to provide shade (4:6), and then "appointed" a worm to attack Jonah's shade bush so that the God-appointed bush withers in a single day. Fish, storms, shade, bushes, and worms are curious side-bars, but not the story.

Nor is the book about Nineveh "that great city," capital of the super-power of the day, Assyria. God commissions Jonah to go to Nineveh, an "exceedingly large" place (3:3) and terribly wicked (1:2), and when Jonah finally gets there the city sets the gold standard for repentance. The king orders all residents—humans *and animals!*—to don sackcloth, fast from food *and water*, and turn from their evil ways and violence (3:7-9). Not bad for a bunch of pagans. God sees what they are up to and changes His mind about destroying them. And so Nineveh becomes the prime example of how people should respond to the word of the Lord (see Matthew 12:41; Luke 11:32). But still, the book is not about the great city. Nineveh only holds the author's attention for five or maybe even seven verses (3:6-10; 1:2; 3:3) and after their crisis finds resolution, the book continues on for another chapter, an odd ending if this is supposed be all about them. In literary terms, the city is a flat character, the bad-turned-good character who serves to advance the greater plot.

So if the book is not about fish 'n more or Nineveh, what is it about? Big surprise, the book is about Jonah, Jonah's God, and what God is to do with a person who refuses to cooperate with a call from God they don't like. Jonah is good with calls that suit him. In his only other appearance in the Old Testament the writer of Kings gives Jonah credit for speaking the word of the Lord, that God would expand the territory from "Lebo-hamath as far as the Sea of the Arabah," a prediction fulfilled during the time of Jeroboam II (II Kings 14:25). Jonah did not refuse or run from all of God's calls; this message seemed to suit him just fine. But when it comes to Nineveh, he does not object that God can't be serious (like Isaiah), protest five times that he is not the right person for the job (like Moses), or even try to strike a bargain with God (like Jacob). Jonah doesn't say a single syllable; he just gets on a ship going in the opposite direction from God's call (1:3). Now, what are you going to do with that? He not only refuses God's call to go to Nineveh, he will not even cooperate with the way a call narrative is supposed to happen.

By this time in our study we do notice several typical features of a call narrative are absent from or minimized in our text. For example, there is not a word about how God summons Jonah's attention; the word of the Lord just "came to Jonah" (1:1). Burning bush, voice in the night, or vision, it's just not important here. Somehow God gets his attention and disrupts Jonah's life, if only because he will not cooperate. But not much is made of any of this up front. God speaks; Jonah listens; Jonah runs. A crisis does loom in the background, but only in the Lord's sparse introductory words: "their wickedness has come up before me" (1:2). The reader is left to imagine what this means for Nineveh, but it's not too difficult to figure: burnt toast, Sodom and Gomorrah... Nineveh.

> **What is God to do with a person who demands to pick and choose which calls he will accept?**

Jonah's commission *is* clear: "Go at once to Nineveh... and cry out against it" (1:2). God calls Jonah, the prophet, to engage in a prophetic-preaching ministry to Nineveh. We do have a call narrative here, it's just messed up by Jonah's response and for that reason the writer draws all of our attention to this feature of the call. What is God to do with a person who demands to pick and choose which calls he will accept?

Jonah runs. He has no desire to discuss the matter with God or anyone else: I am not going to Nineveh [period] and you can't make me [exclamation mark]. And he is not going for good reason. He knows that if he goes, proclaims the word of the Lord, and they repent, God will change His mind and not destroy them. Jonah knows "that you are a gracious God and merciful, slow to anger, and abounding in steadfast love, and ready to relent from punishing" (4:2). Give Jonah an A+ on his theology exam, he can even teach the class next time! He *knows* God will go easy on them at the slightest hint of remorse or change. And Jonah wants no part in this cockeyed plan, saving Nineveh, the people who threaten his way of life in Israel. Give Jonah a pro-Israel, nationalistic call to predict the expansion of borders and he is all over it. But ask him to help *those* people, a nation who pushes borders in the opposite direction, makes his life difficult—that's just not acceptable, somehow not even Israelite. Forget it, I'm outta here.

Just in case we have not yet caught his attitude—understand it, that is—events on the sea wash the film off our glasses. The Lord hurls a storm on the sea to arrest Jonah's attention; he will not let Jonah (or us) off so easy. But it's not Jonah who responds to God's storm, it's the pagan sailors. As the ship threatens to break up, the sailors do the best they know to do; they throw cargo overboard and cry to their gods. Jonah, meanwhile, is dead asleep (1:5). Amazing to us and to the pagan captain of the ship: How can anyone be so unconcerned, so calloused? The ship is going down and everyone is doing all they can to save themselves and Jonah—everyone except Jonah. Nero fiddles, Jonah sleeps. *At least pray to your god*, the captain orders him (1:6), but Jonah would rather die first.

The sailors continue to do all they can. Israelite theologians they are not, but even pagans can see this storm is not normal. So they cast lots to determine who is to blame, and the lot points to Jonah. Caught with no place to run, with a flourish Jonah proclaims his identity as a True Believer in "the Lord, the God of heaven, who made the sea and the dry land" (1:9) and tells them what he is doing on this cruise. And while his hypocrisy doesn't seem to concern him, the sailors are scared out of their wits (1:10). The storm is tossing them around on the sea like a fishing bobber; the ship is breaking up, they are going down. And even when Jonah tells them what they need to do to save themselves, throw him overboard, they refuse to do it. They row hard, try even all the more to save themselves and Jonah (1:13). The irony is stronger than the storm: the divinely called Israelite prophet who refuses to give a few weeks of his time for thousands in Nineveh to have a chance at life and the pagan sailors who at risk of life refuse to give him up for fish bait. Isn't it embarrassing when the pagans possess more of God's heart for people than God's chosen people?

In desperation the sailors toss Jonah overboard, the sea calms, they fear the Lord even more, sacrifice and make vows (1:16). Despite himself, Jonah brings people to the Lord; the sailors convert. And like the sailors, Jonah also prays in the belly of the fish, but read closely and be careful of what we assume. We would like to think, and many do conclude, that after a near-death experience, Jonah would be a changed man and that his prayer is evidence of a penitent prophet ready to turn his life back to God. Lesson learned the hard way.

I don't see the evidence. Jonah prays; he recounts his brush with death, God casting him into the sea (2:3), his desperate cry that he is about to die and never again see God's holy temple (2:4). He describes nearly drowning (2:5). But as his life faded, he appealed to the Lord (2:1,7) and the Lord saved him via the fish. Now he promises to bring thank-offerings and pay his vows: "Deliverance belongs to the Lord!" (2:9). Of course while he is at it he manages to get in a strong right jab at the men who tried to save his life: "Those who worship vain idols forsake their true loyalty" (2:8). All of this is in his prayer, but not a word of contrition in a single line. Jonah is grateful not to be dead, but he is not sorry for refusing God's call. He still has no intention of going to Nineveh should he ever get out of this mess. No, in his prayer Jonah is happy that God saved his life, but that's it. Amen and pass the tartar sauce.

Once the fish cannot stomach him any longer, and God lets the fish off, Jonah still does not clean up and head for Nineveh (3:1-2). God has to call him a second time. And while Jonah goes, it is not because he wants to or has had some change of heart. He goes because he has to, at least he has learned that much from his gastronomic experience. But there is more than one way to counter God's call; if I can't run, then I can sabotage the plan.

Jonah does exactly what God tells him to do; he goes and he preaches—and what a sermon: "Forty days more, and Nineveh shall be overthrown" (3:4). You people are toast. You've got forty days to put your affairs in order, but that's it. You're doomed, deal with it.

Perhaps I'm too hard on Jonah. I'll admit that I can't hear his tone or see the expression on his face after all these years. Maybe he was doing exactly what God wanted in the way God wanted it done. But I doubt it; all indicators point against it. Jonah's sermon offers no word of hope, nothing about repentance or how God might spare them. All these are the pagan king's ideas, not Jonah's. And when the king turns out to be right and their repentance turns the Lord's heart, Jonah goes ballistic. God may have made Jonah preach, but he does it with clenched teeth and a passion to see them burn.

I told you so, Jonah says to the Lord. I "knew that you are a gracious God and merciful, slow to anger, and abounding in steadfast love, and ready to relent from punishing" (4:2). I knew that if I did what you asked and they responded at all, you would go soft. So I ran, should've kept running, but you wouldn't allow that, would you? Okay, so now I have done what you asked, I told them they were going to burn. And now you change your ever-loving mind. How do you think that makes me look? I'll tell you—you've made me look like a fool, like one of the false prophets. Why don't you just kill me and put me out of my misery? (4:3, paraphrased).

"Is it right for you to be angry," God asks. But Jonah does not respond. Instead, he goes outside of town, far enough away not to get hit with any stray fire or brimstone—one can still hope for the best. And he sets up a comfortable cheering section. Now we'll see what God will do, whose side God will take (4:5).

Nineveh is a bit far inland to appoint another fish for Jonah, so God works with a shade bush, a fierce worm, and a sultry east wind (4:6-8). Jonah loves the shade bush, is grateful for the relief from the burning sun. But he is furious with God over the worm and the wind. What kind of God cares so little about me that He would let, no, cause me to suffer in this heat? I'm one of your chosen people and you treat me this way? What kind of sadistic, self-centered, uncaring God are you? Just let me die (4:8).

God continues to work on Jonah: you're close, but you just don't get it. You loved your bush, even though you had no responsibility for it. It just came and went. To tell the truth, you are really just in love with yourself. If something makes you happier, more comfortable, builds your national economy or security, then you are all for it. But if not, you would rather die than look beyond yourself. What if I were like you? What kind of God would I be if I didn't care about the others, Nineveh and all those children? The end.

The call of Jonah is good news if we can hear it. Good news because God's call does not rely on the cooperation or perfection of the one called. The Lord doesn't call Jonah because he has his act together or because God knows Jonah has a heart for missions and will be eager to help. Jonah has a one-track heart for himself and his people; he has no desire to help anyone outside his circle. But God calls him anyway, a divine sense of humor, if you wish, or just divine determination to change Jonah and Nineveh. And God succeeds in Jonah's work with the sailors and the citizens despite his best efforts to thwart God's call. That's good news for Nineveh and for those of us who are far less than we should be on the scales of cooperation and a heart-like-God.

But it's not all good news. Here's the problem with the call of Jonah: I don't know anyone who identifies with Jonah, only those who side against him. His story is so over-the-top we all agree that his response to God's call is terrible, awful, against the heart of God and the life of a believer. Who dares to screen God's calls and accept only the calls that fit with what works for me? Who would dare lecture God about who God should care about (unless it's about me)? Who would allow their comfort, their way of life, their nationalism determine which calls to obey, which to ignore, which to thwart?

Do you see the problem? We can't imagine anyone like Jonah—and we can't see how much, all too often, we are just like him. I need to paint with giant brush strokes here, exceptions will abound and you can discern where the colors are true and when they exaggerate and miss the mark. But let's abandon our safe place outside Nineveh long enough to see ourselves and our churches as others might see us who read our story centuries

> **We can't imagine anyone like Jonah—and we can't see how much, all too often, we are just like him.**

from now. What will they think when they see church budgets with larger line items for new carpet and paint than missions? Five-year church plans to reach this and that group, but not those people who fill our cities but aren't like us? Urban flight so that we can support the ministries we want, to socio-economic groups like ours, instead of hearing calls to minister to the people who drain us and offer nothing in return? Will they see blind nationalistic agendas eager to wave the flag in worship and support the welfare of the state, but ignore or even thwart the needs of those who threaten our way of life? Will they see a church more concerned with her comfort and security than any call to the undesirables whose inclusion might make us uncomfortable?

I paint it large, you can work through the exceptions and special circumstances. But let's not play Jonah and excuse ourselves out of God's call to our generation. The wonderful news, for me, is how like Jonah, we often succeed in God's call despite ourselves. But I wonder what would happen if instead of screening, running from, or sabotaging God's calls, we denied ourselves, picked up a cross and went to Nineveh?

Discussion Questions:

1. Do you know anyone like Jonah who has desperately but unsuccessfully tried to avoid God's call? Share their story. Has this ever happened to you? Explain.

2. Do you think Jonah's experience on the ship and belly of the fish changed him at all? Explain. Have you ever had a near-death experience? Did it change you in any way? How? For how long?

3. Read Philippians 1:15-18. Once Jonah went to Nineveh, did he preach the message God intended for him to preach in the way God wanted him to preach it? What would Paul say about Jonah's reluctant preaching? About our reluctant actions?

4. Compare Jonah's words in 4:2 to Exodus 34:6-7. What do you notice about the relationship of these texts? How do you explain it? How do you account for Jonah's actions in view of his knowledge of this text?

5. Have you ever observed non-Christians (like the sailors) acting with greater integrity or fervency to help others than Christians (like Jonah)? Share your experience. Why does this happen? What can we do to change these situations?

6. What nations, ethnic groups, or others are most like Nineveh to our society? Explain your choices. What is God's call to you regarding these groups? Is this difficult for you? Why or why not?

chapter 10

Mary and Zechariah: Great Expectations

Luke 1:5-38

Three categories of divine call—human response have emerged in our study: great expectations, who would have ever thought it possible, and somewhere in-between. I'd only put Moses, Joshua, and Jonah in the category of *great expectations* of receiving a call from God; Moses because of his time and experience in Egypt, Joshua because of his time with Moses, and Jonah because he was already a prophet (and aren't prophets supposed to receive calls?). Abraham, Sarah, and Jacob belong in the *who would have ever thought it possible* that God would call them category. Abraham and Sarah worshiped other gods in another land; Jacob was—well, Jacob. Others fall *somewhere in-between*: Isaiah and Saul. We're not shocked that God called them, but we can't say that we saw it coming either.

The professor in me demands that we begin this chapter with a test. Don't worry, its only one question, multiple choice: Who is God most likely to call and who is most likely to embrace God's call on their life? A) Mary, a girl in Nazareth, B) Zechariah, a priest on duty in Jerusalem, or C) Beauregard, my basset hound (who appears on all of my multiple choice exams, although he is never the correct answer). The students protest: Not fair, it's a trick question. Perhaps, it all depends on our expectations.

Zechariah is the hands down favorite both to receive and embrace God's call. He's an older man (1:7), and a holy man at that, a priest with the privilege of serving at the temple in Jerusalem (1:8). The writer even goes out of his way to point out that Zechariah and his wife Elizabeth were "righteous before God, living blamelessly according to all the commandments and regulations of the Lord" (1:6). And this particular year Zechariah was even chosen by lot to enter the sanctuary and offer incense in the holy place (1:9). If anyone was ever going to receive a call from God, this is the person and this is the place.

Not Mary. At the very best she's the long shot, but truth be told, for most of us she's not even in the race. She's just a woman and hardly even that, just a young unmarried girl (1:27). Mary's not from the holy city either, but from Nazareth (1:26), the place about which Nathaniel will say what everyone thinks, "Can anything good come out of Nazareth?" (John 1:46). Wrong side of the tracks, wrong gender, wrong age, wrong marital status—from a first century perspective and even most twenty first century perspectives, there is not a chance that God would call her and even less of a chance that she would embrace it if it came.

God's call comes to Zechariah just as we expect. He is in the holy place, doing holy business as close to the divine as a priest dares to go. Outside, the assembly prays (1:10). Inside, Zechariah steps into a small candle-lit room with no windows, one entrance/exit, and only three pieces of furniture: a candle stand, a table, and an incense altar. Otherwise the room is vacant, at least it better be—it is supposed to be. Sure, everyone knows that this is "God's house," but no one really expects God to be home, at least Zechariah didn't. So when the angel of the Lord stepped up beside the incense altar that Zechariah was tending, Zechariah jumped like a kid at a midnight showing of *Friday the Thirteenth*, part thirteen. The writer delicately explains that "he was terrified; and fear overwhelmed him" (1:12). My take is that the only reason he did not run pale faced and screaming holy terror out of the temple was that his feet would not move; he was scared stiff.

The angel tries to calm him and explain his presence. God has heard his prayers and is about to bless him and his wife with a son, an exceptional child. Their son will turn many in Israel back to the Lord and, with the power of the great prophet Elijah, he will "make ready a people prepared for the Lord" (1:16-17). It's a call that, in many respects is nothing more than a glorified birth announcement: "Your wife Elizabeth will bear you a son... You will have joy and gladness, and many will rejoice at his birth" (1:13-14). Congratulations, you are going to be a father!

But God's call does commission Zechariah to take action. First, he must name the son John, "God is gracious" (1:13), against the tradition of naming children after relatives (1:61). Second, he and John's mother must raise the boy as a Nazirite, a person especially set apart to serve God (see Numbers 6:1-21). And to denote his status, the angel specifies that John must never drink any wine or strong drink (1:15). Third, implicit rather than explicit, Zechariah must believe the messenger and trust that God will do as God has promised: Trust me.

What happens next is a bit hard to follow. By every expectation, the "righteous before God" blameless priest at work in the holy place should embrace God's call. If he doesn't, who ever would? But we also know how call narratives work, or at least how they worked in the Old Testament. So we also expect Zechariah to object and to have the right to voice the obvious difficulties with the commission. Abraham, in similar circumstances objected, so did Moses, Isaiah, and Jeremiah. And so Zechariah balks: "How will I know that this is so? For I am an old man, and my wife is getting on in years" (1:18). It's just as the narrator has already explained and everyone already knows; Zechariah and Elizabeth have no children because she is barren and they are both getting on in years (1:7), an all too obvious dif-

ficulty. But then again, we've come to expect some major obstacle to
all of God's calls. A call would not be a call without one.

But our expectations catch us at every turn of this story. In
response to an objection, we know from our study that what is supposed to come next is a reassuring word from God that responds to
the problem, reiterates the call or commission, and may even provide a sign of divine favor. Zechariah gets none of this. Instead, the
angel is frustrated and irritated:

> "I am Gabriel. I stand in the presence of God, and I have
> been sent to speak to you and to bring you this good news.
> But now, because you did not believe my words, which will
> be fulfilled in their time, you will become mute, unable to
> speak, until the day these things occur" (1:19-20).

Gabriel is personally offended that Zechariah would dare to
doubt him and his message. How dare you? You want a sign? I'll give
you a sign: be mute, unable to speak until what I said would happen
happens. Take that.

In view of the typical pattern of a call narrative, Gabriel's reaction
seems a bit extreme. Maybe there was something in Zechariah's tone
that caused him to respond so harshly. Maybe he knew something
about Zechariah's heart; he doesn't believe Gabriel is God's messenger or that God will do any of this. Maybe I am just missing some
clue in the text that would explain his lashing out at Zechariah. Or
maybe, like us, Gabriel's expectation was that this holy man of God,
so close to God's presence in the sanctuary would immediately
embrace God's call on his life, that he would be like Isaiah, eager to
be a part of God's work. But he isn't and when he does not respond
as we expect, it's too disappointing to take.

Months later God sends Gabriel on another house call. Mary is so
not Zechariah, betrothed but not married, a virgin girl no more than

a young teen living in backwater Galilee (1:26-27). She's no priest, never going to be selected by lot to enter the sanctuary, and not in the middle of doing holy business. No offense, but she is just a kid and not since Jacob has there been a candidate less likely to receive a call from God. Who would have ever thought God would call her?

Gabriel startles Mary, more with his words than his presence: "Greetings, favored one! The Lord is with you" (1:28). To which she is "perplexed," puzzled by the strange words (1:29). This can't be right, has to be a case of mistaken identity, a wrong address. Favored one? Maybe by Joseph, my parents, but who else would *favor me*? The Lord is with you? Me? The Lord is not with me; I'm just Mary, a girl in Nazareth. What could this person be thinking? (Does she realize who this is yet?)

Gabriel calms her and explains. And like his speech to Zechariah, in many respects his call is no more than a glorified birth announcement. Glorified indeed:

> Do not be aftraid, Mary, for you have found favor with God. And now, you will conceive in your womb and bear a son, and you will name him Jesus. He will be great, and will be called the Son of the Most High, and the Lord God will give to him the throne of his ancestor David. He will reign over the house of Jacob forever, and of his kingdom there will be no end. (1:30-33)

Some birth announcement: You will conceive and deliver the Son of God who will take the throne of David and reign forever over a kingdom with no limits. I just need you to do two things. One, name the child Jesus, "the Lord saves" (1:31), because that's His life's mission. Two, trust me. Dare to believe that you have found favor with God and don't be afraid (1:30). No problems, Mary, trust me.

There is, of course, one slight problem—at least from a medical, social, psychological, marital, familial, and theological point of view. Mary replies (does she know his identity yet?), "How can this be, since I am a virgin?" (1:34). The narrative has already emphasized the point in every prior reference to her: God sent Gabriel to "the virgin" engaged to Joseph (1:27a) and "the virgin's name was Mary" (1:27e). Roll up into one big objection all of the other objections from every call God every extended and it is still no contest. At least old Abraham had a wife, Jacob had

> **The one we least expect God to call embraces an assignment that will change her life, and not all for the good.**

old Abraham had a wife, Jacob had prospects, and Moses could put two words together. Mary is a virgin—has been and will remain so— yet will conceive a son. She has the Everest of all objections, and wins by a landslide.

Maybe that's why Gabriel responds to her so differently than he did to Zechariah. He offers reassurance that explains how such a thing could be possible. The Holy Spirit, the power of the Most High will come to you; the father of the child will be God himself (1:35). And for a sign, even barren Elizabeth has conceived a child with Zechariah and is six months along (1:36). You see, Mary, "Nothing will be impossible with God" (1:37). And Mary, the kid from Galilee, steals Isaiah's line—and more, "Here am I, the servant of the Lord; Let it be with me according to your word" (1:38).

The one we least expect God to call embraces an assignment that will change her life, and not all for the good. There will have to be explanations—to her parents, to Joseph, to his parents. Her credibility in the community is at stake, probably already shot. Rumors will fly from the narrow streets of Nazareth to the open fields of Galilee. Nothing about this will be easy, even her life will be at risk in childbirth. And still, it's what she cannot imagine about this call that will be the hardest to swallow: what the crowds will say about her boy, "He has a demon and is out of his mind" (John 10:20); what He will say about her, "Who is my mother, and who are my brothers?" and then pointing to the disciples say, "Here are my mother and my brothers!" (Matthew 12:48-49) or "Whoever loves father or mother more than me is not worthy of me; and whoever loves son or daughter more than me is not worthy of me" (Matthew 10:37). And then at the foot of a Roman cross, standing, watching the child of promise tortured, dying—and the God who called nowhere to be found: My God! My God! Why have you forsaken him? (cf. Matthew 27:46).

But still, the one we least expect grasps God's call with both hands while the one who should receive and embrace the good news of a son in his old age, the gospel of God's in-breaking kingdom, this one doubts. The older man can't imagine how God could turn back the clock and reverse barrenness into new life. It's illogical foolishness. The young girl can only imagine how she will remain a virgin and bear the son of God, but she believes and submits her life to God's plan. The righteous holy man with nothing to lose in the deal balks, while the unmarried kid puts everything— marriage, family, happiness, life itself—everything at risk.

It's time for a post-class quiz. Again no worries, only one question, multiple-choice, I'll even leave Beauregard in the doghouse: Who do we identify with in these stories? A) Zechariah, the righteous holy man with a long track record with God in his life, or B) Mary, the young girl with little experience of God. Same question, reworded: How do I respond to God's call on my life? A) Like Zechariah, so settled into the *status quo* of religion, even if it is a bit barren at least it is safe from wild new directions that topple everything upside down, or B) Like Mary, so far removed from status and so full of faith that she is open to whatever God has in mind.

Each generation seems to partake in a common meal of bemoaning the state of the faith in the hands of the next generation. If we believe the press, the future of the church is sliding head-first down the slope to hell, greased slick with the heresies of the young. They are careless with traditional concerns, weak on doctrines that in our lifetime have split our churches like a two-ton log splitter set on automatic. With seeming disregard they throw off long held practices and replace them with new methods, small groups instead of Sunday night assembly, house churches instead of buildings, you name it—they'll try it! This generation doesn't share our vision for the church! And from where I sit in college classrooms, it's absolutely true. They don't share our vision—and thank God! Thank God that their vision is so much broader and their faith open, so much more like Mary's than Zechariah's.

My students shame me. I am Zechariah in a generation of Marys. I'm the professor, chair of a Christian University Bible department, years of experience in ministry, hundreds of sermons under my belt, thousands of Bible classes. But I'm the one left standing mute inside the temple while my students embrace God's call with arms wide open to the possibilities. They are the ones who spend Saturday mornings and Sunday afternoons walking the neighborhoods praying, serving, being salt and light. They are the ones moving from the suburbs to the inner-city ministries in Forth Worth, Denver, Los Angeles, and Miami. This generation spends their spring breaks and vacation time traveling to third world countries instead of five star hotels. They build houses, schools, and church buildings. They drill water-wells in Africa, conduct medical clinics in remote mountain villages of Central America, and teach Christ everywhere they go. They embody the mission of Jesus: "The Spirit of the Lord is upon me, because he has anointed me to bring good news to the poor. He has sent me to proclaim release to the captives and recovery of sight to the blind, to let the oppressed go free, to proclaim the year of the Lord's favor" (Luke 4:18-19; cf. Isaiah 61:1-2).

This generation has a passion unsurpassed by any before, but not a passion to tend the fortress of the church. Their dream is nothing less than busting down the walls and going out to the world to serve in the name of Jesus. Somewhere, somehow, this generation has heard this call and is rising up like Mary, willing to put their lives at risk for the plan of God. They are the service generation and I think the future of the kingdom of God is in good hands, and will remain so as long as we can keep Zechariah out of the way. If we can resist the paternal urge to infect them with a version of the faith that offers incense, pure in orthodoxy, but can't seem to embrace a bigger, riskier vision of the kingdom of God, one that might cost us our status, our security, or even our lives, then in time, maybe like Zechariah in this story, we too will come around to take up God's call.

Discussion Questions:

1. What is the crisis or crises to which God's call of Zechariah and Mary responds? How important is their reception of God's call in the resolution of these crises? Explain.

2. How did you respond to the first quiz? Would you normally expect Mary or Zechariah to receive and embrace God's call? Why? What do our expectations express about our understanding of God? What does God's call to both of them teach us about God?

3. This chapter stresses the differences between Mary and Zechariah. In what ways are they alike? Explain. How are these similarities important for receiving God's call?

4. Do you know anyone like Mary or Zechariah? Share their stories. How would you have expected them to respond to God's call? How do you think you would have responded in their situation? Are you a Mary or Zechariah?

5. Why do you think Gabriel was so hard on Zechariah? Why did he not treat Mary in the same way? Explain. What does this teach us about God's expectations of us?

6. Reflect on the call narratives we have studied thus far. Do those with the most experience of God generally have more trouble responding to God's call than those with less experience? Explain. In view of your response, do you agree or disagree that younger Christians (in maturity, not physical age) tend to be more like Mary while older Christians tend to be more like Zechariah? Explain.

chapter 11

Samuel: Who's There?

1 Samuel 3:1-18

By this point in our study I hope we have established two fundamental ideas. First, the basic responsibility of the "called" is to trust the God who calls and step out in faith. This first step has been a literal one for many: a step toward the Promised Land (Abraham and Sarah), a step back to Egypt (Moses), a step into the river (Joshua), a step into Nineveh (Jonah). God's call never leaves a person standing where they were, if it did what would be the point of the call? Rather, God calls people to change—whether that change is where they go and what they do or their relationship to God, or both. And any significant life change demands trust in the one who asks us to change, trust that God knows what He is doing, that God cares about what is best for us, and that God is capable of keeping His end of the bargain.

Second, the responsibility for placing a successful call belongs to God, not us. We need not wait by the phone for fear of missing God's call. God sets the ring tone as loud as needed: visions, burning bushes, and blinding light, or as soft as the voice of a mentor. He even has call roaming with impeccable clarity from Ur of the Chaldees to the wilderness of Sinai and all points between. We do not need to worry about God getting through. See point one: trust the God who calls.

But with this said (again), I cannot put off THE question any longer. I would like to; and I warn that you will not be satisfied with my answer. I am not satisfied with it myself. Here it is: So how do we identify the call of God today? My friend Linda provided me with an excellent synopsis of the question from a class discussion:

> The Taliban think they hear God's call; so do the levitating Buddhist monks, the Shiite militia, president Bush, the Aryan brotherhood... (People were not saying those are all equivalent.) So... how can we KNOW that it is God who is calling us?

I think of movies. What makes the voice Ray Kinsella hears in *Field of Dreams* ("If you build it they will come") better than the voice John Nash imagines in *A Beautiful Mind*? Is it that others are eventually caught up in Ray's delusion while John is never able to convince anyone? Is it because doctors diagnose and treat John Nash as a paranoid schizophrenic while Ray's family never commits him? Indeed, how does one discern the voice of God from other voices?

Only one call narrative in Scripture exhibits any concern for this question, and even here, not much is made of the problem. Nonetheless, at least Samuel's story gives us some opportunity to explore our question and see how the problem is resolved in at least this instance. The story begins with "The word of the Lord was rare in those days; visions were not wide-

How does one discern the voice of God from other voices?

spread" (I Samuel 3:1). It's the equivalent of a playwright setting a loaded gun on the nightstand in the opening act; before the curtain comes down the gun will go off. So we can be sure that before our story is over there will be a vision with the word of the Lord. Perhaps more important is how the gun came to be loaded; why was the word of the Lord so rare in those days?

First Samuel continues the storyline from the book of Judges. Here, Israelite society is in a tailspin. Episode after episode from across Israel tell the same story: the people abandon the Lord and turn to local gods, the Lord hands them over to punishment from nations, desperate and helpless the people cry out to the Lord for help, the Lord cannot stand to see His people suffer and so delivers them by means of a "judge" (a hero), and then after the death of the judge the people repeat the cycle (Judges 2:11-19; e.g., 3:7-12). This dismal sequence is the story of Judges 1-16: now in the land, God's people are in full self-destruct mode. And it's not just the "landed" tribes, not just the laity who are melting down, but the Levites too, the priestly tribe. This collapse of faith is the theme of the final chapters of Judges (17-21); and even Stephen King would have difficulty imagining the horrors the writer depicts here: Levite priests selling their services to the highest bidder and god of choice (17:1-18:31), an Israelite town doing their best imitation of Sodom but settling for the gang rape of a woman instead of a man (19:10-26), a priest chopping up his concubine wife into twelve pieces just to send a message (19:27-21:7), civil war (20:8-48), more killing, more abductions, more rape (21:1-25). No wonder the word of the Lord was rare in those days.

Closer to 1 Samuel 3, the priesthood at the tabernacle in Shiloh was as corrupt as any modern televangelist. Eli's sons, Hophni and Phineas, skimmed off the top of the sacrifices, although exactly how is difficult to figure from the text (I Samuel 2:12-17). An occasional worshiper might try to stop them, but threats of violence kept things in order and the best food on their tables (2:16). Of course there was the sex, apparently lots of it with the women who served at the tabernacle (2:22). And it's not surprising that these two priests shared the common perception that the Lord was pretty much contained to

His throne on the Ark of the Covenant, kind of a god-in-a-box men-
tality. Just like the sacrifices and the women, Hophni and Phineas
controlled this god: manipulate as needed, haul Him out to win a
battle and then put Him back in His room (4:1-11).

We want Eli to be the hero, the devout priest who stands by his
convictions in the middle of it all. But he's not. He knows what his
sons are doing with the women and about the sacrifice scam. He
talks to Hophni and Phineas, warns them, but he doesn't stop them
(2:22-25). Maybe he fails because the Lord had already decided to
kill them (2:25), but the Lord still holds him responsible (3:13).
Complicity, not convictions, rules the day. Eugene Peterson's summary is harsh, but accurate:

> [Eli] has turned into a parody of a priest: religion is his job,
> his priestly calling reduced to a religious function; he doesn't
> have to deal with God at all (1:14). Hophni and Phineas are
> also parody-priests, only worse; the holy place for them is a
> place of power and privilege—access to easy women and
> gourmet food. God is the last thing on their minds... Holy
> places provide convenient cover for unholy ambitions—they
> always have, and they always will. (*First and Second Samuel*,
> 37-38)

No wonder the word of the Lord was uncommon; the only marvel is that the Lord's word came often enough for the writer to cate-
gorize it as a rare event.

Samuel was just a young boy stuck in the middle of all this. His
mother, Hannah, had dedicated him to the Lord before his birth and
since left him at the Shiloh tabernacle to minister under Eli's supervi-
sion (2:11; please tell me that she didn't know what was going on at
Shiloh). And it is the kid who becomes the counter-point to the corruption. While Hophni and Phineas run up the expense account,

Samuel "was ministering before the Lord" (2:18). While the brothers sleep around with the church secretaries, Samuel "grew up in the presence of the Lord" (2:21). And while the father fails and God determines to kill the clergy, "Samuel continued to grow both in stature and in favor with the Lord and with people" (2:26, cf. Luke 2:52).

So we return to the beginning: the boy Samuel is ministering to the Lord under Eli and the word of the Lord is rare (3:1), and we understand both the crisis and why God's next move is to call the kid to be His prophet.

> At that time Eli, whose eyesight had begun to grow dim so that he could not see, was lying down in his room; the lamp of God had not yet gone out, and Samuel was lying down in the temple of the Lord, where the ark of God was. Then the Lord called, "Samuel! Samuel!" and he said, "Here I am!" and ran to Eli, and said, "Here I am, for you called me." But he said, "I did not call; lie down again." So he went and lay down. The Lord called again, "Samuel!" Samuel got up and went to Eli, and said, "Here I am, for you called me." But he said, "I did not call, my son; lie down again." Now Samuel did not yet know the Lord, and the word of the Lord had not yet been revealed to him. The Lord called Samuel again, a third time. And he got up and went to Eli, and said, "Here I am, for you called me." Then Eli perceived that the Lord was calling the boy. Therefore Eli said to Samuel, "Go, lie down; and if he calls you, you shall say, 'Speak, Lord, for you servant is listening.'" So Samuel went and lay down in his place. (1 Samuel 3:2-9)

The text is the literary equivalent of chocolate covered cherries, first appearances only slightly conceal layers of meaning. Eli's spiritual blindness is matched by deterioration of his physical sight (3:2). Night has fallen on Israel and the tabernacle, but God's lamp has not yet died (3:3). A flicker of hope still burns for Israel—inside the tabernacle where Samuel lies in close proximity to the divine, maybe even closer than orthodoxy would like (3:3, was Samuel in the holy of holies with the ark? See Leviticus 16:2). Yet the boy who would be a prophet does not yet "know" the Lord; he does not recognize the Lord's voice, he has never heard it before (3:7). Three times God speaks his name, "Samuel!" but no charm. Instead, it is the blind man who figures it out, who perceives that it must be the Lord and instructs his young disciple on proper etiquette with the divine.

God did not have trouble getting Samuel's attention. A night voice in what should be an empty tabernacle takes care of that. The difficulty was getting him to realize who was trying to get his attention, that it was God and not a human. Finally, it was Eli, his spiritual mentor, corrupt and fallible, who did his job, and identified the voice and made the introduction. Go back, lie down, and wait. If he calls again, tell the Lord you're ready to listen.

So Samuel receives God's call. The Lord again summons his attention ("Samuel! Samuel!") and he acknowledges himself as the Lord's servant (3:10). What follows, the announcement of God's judgment on Eli and his family (3:11-14), presupposes that this message to Samuel commissions him as God's prophet. In other words, instead of explicitly commissioning Samuel to be a prophet (e.g., like Jeremiah, "you shall speak whatever I command you" [Jeremiah 1:7]), God commands Samuel what he will speak and, thus, implicitly calls him to be a prophet.

Samuel knows this. The next morning he hesitates to get up (his version of an objection) because he knows that Eli (and God) expects him to relay God's message (3:15). And it is Eli who provides the words of reassurance, albeit more threatening than affirming, that Samuel must carry out his call despite his reluctance: "Do not hide it from me. May God do so to you and more also, if you hide anything from me of all that he told you" (3:17). So, Samuel answers God's call; he speaks the word of the Lord to Eli—all of it (3:18).

The epilogue of the story confirms that a prophetic call has just come to Samuel. All Israel comes to know that Samuel is a trustworthy prophet of the Lord (3:20) and what was a rare event, the word of the Lord coming to the people (3:1), is no longer rare. The Lord continues to appear to Samuel at Shiloh and the word of Samuel/the Lord came to all Israel (3:21-4:1). The gun on the nightstand has fired. God has called a prophet to Israel.

So we return to the question, how do we know when God is calling us? I limit my response here to a few observations based on Samuel's story and save further reflection for our next chapter. First, a direct call from God was rare in ancient Israel, no more than a couple of handfuls over the span of a thousand or more years. The narrator of Samuel says this was exceptionally true prior to Samuel's call, "the word of the Lord was rare in those days" (I Samuel 3:1). But at no time was God's call common or the norm. I suppose our study, by collecting the call narratives, viewing them side by side, and emphasizing this theme in Scripture, may promote the misperception that God calls someone everyday in grandiose fashion. Not so. Direct, in-your-face, burning-bush versions of God's call are historically rare in ancient Israel, even if a major theme in Scripture. They are the exceptional moments at key intersections of Israelite and world history and for this reason they were preserved in the text, not because they were common occurrences. So a caution is in order: beware of attempts to turn what was exceptional into a commonplace event in the life of every believer.

When God decides to call a person, God will get through.

Second, when God decides to call a person, God will get through. You may be weary of me repeating this, but I'm not. God had to call

Samuel four times before Samuel finally realized it was the Lord. And I suspect the Lord would have kept calling his name all night long that night, the next, and the next... until Samuel caught on. If God has a call for a person's life, God has the patience and persistence to make His voice clear and recognizable. Again, we can relax and, like Samuel, focus on the ministry God has already set in front of us.

Third, spiritual mentors, even fallible ones like Eli (the only kind there are) may discern God's call on our lives better than we can. "Eli perceived that the Lord was calling the boy" (I Samuel 3:8). Explain it as you wish—mentors know our strengths, weaknesses and talents, they bring perspective to the situation, they have experience to evaluate when a thing is of God or not—and God uses mentors to identify or even place calls: Moses to Joshua, Paul to Timothy, Eli to Samuel.

> **No one called by God in Scripture, so far as I can tell, wanted the task God gave them.**

Fourth, another caution: beware of receiving the "call" that you always wanted. No one called by God in Scripture, so far as I can tell, wanted the task God gave them. No one. They did what God asked and maybe even came to embrace it, but they did not aspire or hope for such calls. Quite the opposite. God's call asks the unthinkable: go to Nineveh, leave your home, scrap your life and start over, tell Eli his family is doomed. May I be blunt on this point? I am amazed by how many ministers are "called" by God to go to larger churches with higher salaries while so few are "called" to move in the opposite direction. Now I am not saying that moving to a larger church with a better salary is wrong, but let's be careful of our language. If we really want God's call it will more likely take us where we never dreamed and don't want to go. At least that's the way it worked in the call narratives we have been studying. And yet we do not lose heart, but we rejoice because it was in the middle of such an undesirable call and circumstance Paul reminds us that we can "do all things through him who strengthens me" (Philippians 4:13).

Finally, we would do well to remember that what we have in the biblical text are reflections on past events confirmed by later experience, not a live action report. In other words, Abraham, Moses, Samuel and the others may have, and I suspect did, wonder if they had lost their marbles when God first called. So we ask how did they *know at the moment it happened*? And I think we have to respond that they probably didn't *know*, at least not at first. Later, yes perhaps, but only when the course of their life offered confirmation. Like it or not, we are not dealing with a science experiment, slice it open, put it under a microscope and provide conclusive proof. Sorry, but try as we might to turn the spiritual life into modern science, the inscrutability of a relationship with the divine does not work that way.

I warned you that you would be disappointed, but that's the most I can say from this text. Direct calls are rare in Scripture and when they do come, God persists and spiritual mentors help until the one called gets it. Even then the called may not *know* anything for sure, except that they never would have chosen this task for themselves. Indirect calls, a category we have not yet defined or discussed, are somewhat different—and to these calls we turn in our next chapter.

Discussion Questions:

1. Do you think Hannah was aware of the true situation at the tabernacle in Shiloh? Why or why not? If she was aware, why do you think she left Samuel? If she was not, do you think she would have left Samuel had she known? What do these responses say about her relationship to God?

2. We seem to hear news of corrupt clergy on a regular basis. Why do those closest to the "holy" (e.g., tabernacle, church) often become so corrupt? What is it about their position that promotes moral decay? If you are a paid minister, what safeguards or precautions do you have in place to prevent such corruption in your life?

3. Why did Samuel not recognize God's voice? Why did he think it was Eli calling him?

4. Have you ever consulted a mentor or close friend for insight into God's will for your life? Share your story. How would you compare your experience to Eli's relationship with Samuel?

5. Samuel relays God's decision to destroy Eli's priesthood. Fulfillment of this prophecy began immediately (see I Samuel 4:12-22) but was not complete until approximately 100 years later, well after Samuel's death (see I Kings 2:26-27). In view of this delay do you think Samuel wondered about the authenticity of his call? Do you think others might have questioned his call? Explain.

6. What criteria would you suggest for discerning the call of God? On a scale of one to ten, how would you rate the strength or clarity of each criterion?

chapter 12

Our Christian Calling

Christians are a called people. Days after the Lord's ascension Peter announced forgiveness of sin and the gift of the Holy Spirit to those who would repent and be immersed in the name of Jesus. He explained that "the promise is for you, for your children, and for all who are far away, everyone whom the Lord our God *calls to him*" (Acts 2:39, emphasis mine). Here, Peter makes two points clear: 1) God's call precedes His gifts, anyone who has received the gift of forgiveness and the Spirit had already been called by God, and 2) God's call was not limited to the first century, but active for all future generations.

Paul's letters also assume the called status of every believer. He writes to the church at Corinth:

> To the church of God that is in Corinth, to those who are sanctified in Christ Jesus, *called to be saints*, together with all those who in every place *call* on the name of our Lord Jesus Christ, both their Lord and ours... (I Corinthians 1:2, emphasis mine)

Every believer who *calls* on Jesus has been *called* by God to be one of the holy ones, the saints. This is even more explicit later in the letter when Paul urges the Corinthians to "lead the life that the

Lord has assigned, to which God called you" (7:17). Circumcised or uncircumcised, slave or free, "In whatever condition you were called... there remain with God" (7:18-24). Paul gives the theme more emphasis in his letter to Rome:

> We know that all things work together for good for those who love God, **who are called according to his purpose**. For those whom he foreknew he also predestined to be conformed to the image of his Son, in order that he might be the firstborn within a large family. And those whom he predestined **he also called**; and **those whom he called** he also justified; and those whom he justified he also glorified. (Romans 8:28-30, emphasis mine)

And this sampling just touches the fringe of texts in the New Testament that assert God's calling of Christians. Space prevents consideration of other relevant passages: Romans 9:24; 1 Corinthians 1:9; Galatians 5:8,13; Colossians 3:15; 1 Thessalonians 5:24; 2 Peter 1:3. Whatever else we may conclude, at least this much is clear: Christians are a called people.

An "uncalled" Christian is an impossible contradiction of terms.

Drive this survey marker deep: Just as God called Abraham, Jacob, Joshua and the others, we too are called. Peter, Paul, and the whole of the New Testament witness can't see it any other way. An "uncalled" Christian is an impossible contradiction of terms; Christians become Christians by the call of God—and "the One who calls you is faithful" (I Thessalonians 5:24). But so what? It's a nice sentiment, "a called people," it sounds good. But does our status as called people have any real significance, make any real difference? Paul and other writers seem to think so.

First, the "call" in these texts refers to an invitation to join God's life and purposes in Christ. So, God's call to new life includes the idea of salvation (Acts 2:38; I Timothy 6:12; II Timothy 1:9), but it is not limited to forgiveness. God's call is bigger than a simple equation of call = salvation. Our forgiveness is only the beginning. The gospel calls us into the fellowship of the Son (I Corinthians 1:9) to live out God's purposes, in Romans 8 to live according to the Spirit, not the flesh (Romans 8:12-17), in I Corinthians to be holy (I Corinthians 1:2; see also I Peter 1:15; 2:9-10), in Galatians to live in freedom (Galatians 5:13), in Ephesians to live together in humility and unity (Ephesians 4:1-6), in 1 Peter to follow Christ's example of suffering (I Peter 2:21). God's call is the fulcrum for all of these actions. Our call is nothing less than to be transformed as we join the in-breaking work of the kingdom of heaven.

Second, God calls us to this new life, according to Paul, through the proclamation of the gospel: "he called you through our proclamation of the good news" (II Thessalonians 2:14a). In comparison to the stories we have studied in this volume our call is indirect, through mediators who share the good news with us, extend God's invitation. But it is nonetheless God's call. The Lord's call on Joshua or Timothy was no less "of God" just because God worked through Moses and Paul to summon them. So God's call to people through Peter on Pentecost or Paul on his missions is no less God's call just because it comes through the medium of another person.

> **The Lord's call on Joshua or Timothy was no less "of God" just because God worked through Moses and Paul to summon them.**

Third, one of Paul's greatest concerns is that we live up to our calling. He reminds the church at Thessalonica that in his early work among them he urged and pleaded with them to "lead a life worthy of God, who calls you into his own kingdom and glory" (I

Thessalonians 2:11-12). In the same way, Paul writes in the letter to the Ephesians,

> I therefore, the prisoner of the Lord, beg you to lead *a life worthy of the calling to which you have been called*, with all humility and gentleness, with patience, bearing with one another in love, making every effort to maintain the unity of the Spirit in the bond of peace. There is one body and one Spirit, just as *you were called to the one hope of your calling*, one Lord, one faith, one baptism, one God and Father of all, who is above all and through all and in all. (Ephesians 4:1-6, emphasis mine)

And when Paul sends word back to Galatia he expresses dismay that they "are so quickly deserting the one who called you in the grace of Christ and are turning to a different gospel" (Galatians 1:6). Paul is not worried whether or not God has called the people in Thessalonica, Ephesus, or Galatia. He knows God has called and they have accepted. Paul's concern is whether they will honor their calling and the God who calls.

But there is more. Fourth, God's call on our lives through the gospel also commissions us to our place within the body of Christ. So, as Paul continues in Ephesians 4, the language of "calling" melds into the language of "gifts" for the church:

> [I] beg you to lead a life worthy of the calling to which you have been called... But each of us was given grace according to the measure of Christ's gift... The gifts he gave were that some would be apostles, some prophets, some evangelists, some pastors and teachers, to equip the saints... for building up the body of Christ. (4:1, 7, 11-12)

A life worthy of God's call is one that humbly employs God's gift for the benefit of the whole body of Christ.

The same transition takes place in Romans. After Paul emphasizes in chapter 8 that Christians have been "called according to his [God's] purpose" (8:28), he urges the called not to think more highly of themselves than they ought to think, "but to think with sober judgment, each according to the measure of faith that God has assigned" (12:3b). Although we are all called by God, he explains, we have different gifts. And our responsibility is to put our gifts to use for the greater good: "We have gifts that differ according to the grace given to us: prophecy, in proportion to faith; ministry, in ministering; the teacher, in teaching; the exhorter, in exhortation; the giver, in generosity; the leader, in diligence; the compassionate, in cheerfulness" (12:6-8). Paul also tells those "called to be saints" in Corinth that "there are varieties of gifts, but the same Spirit; and there are varieties of services, but the same Lord; and there are varieties of activities, but it is the same God who activates all of them in everyone. To each is given the manifestation of the Spirit for the common good" (I Corinthians 12:4-7).

> Those called by God, all Christians, are also gifted (called) by God for the welfare of the church.

I recognize that this terminology differs from the word "call" and that some may feel I am stretching the point, but I think the connections are close. Those called by God, all Christians, are also gifted (called) by God for the welfare of the church. On the one level we receive the same call from God; on the other we receive different gifts (calls) for the church. Paul accepts this as a given; his point is that we recognize the entire range of gifts, not just the high profile roles, and that we humbly use our diverse gifts for each other, not ourselves, to build up the body of Christ in unity. Reminiscent of Moses at the bush, God's call/gifting is not about me, stroking my ego, what I want to do, or what I don't want to do; God's call is about greater needs.

This recognition, however, leads us back to the question we began to ponder in the last chapter, *the* question: How can I know God's call on my life? How am I to discern the unique gifts or call God has given me? I want to be responsible, faithful with God's investment. I want to be the five or ten talent person in Jesus' parable, putting God's loan of talent to work and showing a profit (Matthew 25:14-30). But how can I invest my calling, my gifts, if I don't even know what they are? How do I know what God wants me to do?

What we would like, we think, is either a direct word from God ("your call is to preach on the radio") or an indirect word through some sure-fire seven step program. On the former, be careful what you ask for. As we have seen, with rare exceptions, no one who received a direct call from God was happy about what God had to offer. On the latter, while I do not doubt there is some value in programs or questionnaires to discovering your spiritual gifts/call, I am suspicious by nature and experience.

I am curious about what drives us to quick fixes and sure-fire solutions to questions about our calling. For many our motivation is a simple desire to be used by God for the church in the world; we just don't know where to go or what to do and our confusion wants a clear resolution. We want to please God, succeed in our ministry, and feel good about ourselves and our relationship to God. Nothing wrong with any of that. But there are dangers lurking in the shadow of these sentiments. At worst, discerning my call or gift becomes something about me; at the least, the threat of self-centeredness is apparent in all this. Or, figuring out what God wants me to do may be motivated by fear, a fear that if we do not discern our gift or call, God will be peeved with us. What an odd view of God: A God who does not make his call clear but then holds us accountable.

One other danger also prowls in the shadows: I become so consumed with finding my call that I close my eyes to all the needs and opportunities around me. In a perverse sense, my inward navel-gazing to find God's will for my life may become my excuse for not engaging in what God has set in front of my eyes. Instead of this task, I want something more glamorous, a call that rings my bell. As Paul might say, we want to be hands not feet, mouths not little toes (I Corinthians 12). The problem, then, is not discerning God's call; the problem is my pride that only wants a certain type of call.

> **The problem, then, is not discerning God's call; the problem is my pride that only wants a certain type of call.**

Forgive my negativity, but this needs to be said here. Too often, searching for our call or trying to discern our spiritual gifts becomes no more than an excuse for not doing what needs to be done here and now. Mark, a preaching friend of mine, put it this way: Sometimes my calling is just what needs to be done—and I am in a position to do it and can do it. He continued to explain, taking out the garbage or changing dirty diapers is not my "spiritual gift." But pity the man who thinks this excuses him to skip out to the next spiritual discernment conference to discover his call from God. He doesn't need a call from God, he just needs a wake-up call.

With that said, and with caution regarding *hair growth tonic guaranteed to produce results in ten short days*, how may we better discern God's indirect calls? Just a few tentative observations from the text: First, what do you do well or better than anything else? Note, I did not say better than *anyone* else. If comparison to others becomes the standard for a call, no one will ever do anything. What do you do best? In Exodus 31, the Lord tells Moses that he has "called by name Bezalel son of Uri son of Hur, of the tribe of Judah" to produce the artwork and other skilled work for the tabernacle (Exodus 31:1-11). God tells

Moses, but I doubt he spoke direct to Bezalel. So how did he know this was his calling? Simple, he was a master craftsperson in design, metal work, and precious gems. He was a skilled artist. So when the community needed skilled artwork–he was commissioned by God through Moses (along with many other good artisans). So, what are you good at (and despise not the small things)? If we know what we can do well and see a need, what are we waiting for?

Second, what are you passionate about? What stirs your heart and emotion to the point that you must do something? When Nehemiah heard the report about the survivors in Jerusalem with the city wall torn down and no gates to close for security, he says "I sat down and wept, and mourned for days, fasting and praying before the God of heaven" (Nehemiah 1:4). God put the burden of Jerusalem on his heart–and there is nothing mystical about it: a devastating report + a heart sensitive to Jerusalem = a burden from God. I grant that the term "call" does not appear in the book of Nehemiah. The writer never explicitly says "God called Nehemiah" to rebuild the walls of Jerusalem. But God did, without question God called Nehemiah by bringing him news that his heart could not ignore.

Now here's the tricky part: countless thousands also knew the same data about Jerusalem. But this information did not move them in the same way it touched Nehemiah, or at least if it did, they were not in a position to do anything. Nehemiah had both the burden and the opportunity to make a difference. What I am trying to say is that we are all different, we see different needs, respond emotional-ly to different events–and thank God for it! What troubles you to the point of action and what concerns me are likely to be different needs. Amber visited remote Honduras just like many others before and since. But what she saw + her passions = children she could not just walk away from, not when she could do something. There was no vision, no burning bush, no voice from on high, but it is no less God's call.

In some respects, the type of calling we are now talking about parallels the Nazarite vow in ancient Israel. A Nazarite was a "lay" member of Israel, not a priest, prophet, or any other religious official (although they too could elect to take a Nazarite vow). This person, for whatever reason might be in their heart, would especially devote themselves to the Lord for a season of time, not unlike a short term mission. Numbers 6 provides a few stipulations for such a person, but the objective or purpose of their vow is wide-open. In other words, any person, male or female, could "call" themselves to special times of devotion or service to God, I suspect because of some special duty that was on their heart like Nehemiah.

Third, one last idea, if we just don't know what we do best or don't have any passions, after we pinch ourselves to make sure we are not dead, maybe we should turn to the church. In the New Testament the church often bears responsibility for calling people on behalf of God. In Acts 6 the apostles charge the church with identifying "seven men of good standing, full of the Spirit and wisdom" (Acts 6:3). This was not self-selection, but communal identification of those best suited for the task. And as requested, the church turns up seven men whom the apostles appoint with prayer and the laying on of hands. I'd say they have been called.

In the same way Paul instructs Timothy on how to identify suitable shepherds in Ephesus (I Timothy 3) and Titus on the same subject in Crete (Titus 1:5-9). In some fashion, not entirely clear, Timothy, Titus and the churches identified the right people for the task and appointed them. And through this process, the Holy Spirit made these new shepherds overseers (Acts 20:28). Implicitly, God called these elders through the faithful actions of the church.

These are just a few suggestions drawn from what we find in the biblical text: What do we do best? What are our passions, the tender spots easily ignited? What does the church say? I am well aware that this does not resolve all of our questions, but it does send us in the right direction. Most of all, I hope it gets us out of the closet where we spend years trying to figure out God's call before we do anything. Whatever God's call may be, that's not it. We are a called people, now. We need only to open our hearts and our eyes and embrace what is before us.

Discussion Questions:

1. What do you think of the author's distinction between direct and indirect calls? How would you define a direct call? An indirect call?

2. Why do we crave certainty about our calling? In what ways would greater certainty help us or the kingdom of God? In what ways might greater confidence be detrimental?

3. Do you agree with the author's claim that too often our search for God's calling is an excuse not to do what God has already set before us? Explain your position. Has this ever been true for you? Share your story.

4. What are the greatest needs in your community? What do you see? After making a short list, share these with the group. Notice how group members see and identify different needs. Why do you think this is so?

5. If you are discussing this chapter with a group, have the group share what they see are the talents or special gifts of each group member. In what ways do these talents denote God's calling?

chapter 13

When God Calls

Our journey has visited ten episodes of calling scattered over a thousand years across the fertile crescent of the ancient Near East. We've peered over shoulders to catch glimpses of visions that prompted Isaiah to volunteer, Zechariah to hesitate, Jacob to bargain, and Mary to submit. We've tuned our ears to hear God's voice speaking to Moses the contortionist trying to escape God's call, Jonah the track star who decides to run, and Joshua the stalwart who immediately sets to work. And we watched as Samuel mistook God's voice for Eli, Saul was stunned by a voice he never expected to hear or associate with God, and Abraham and Sarah heard God's call and left everything behind.

Our study could continue with more stories, more episodes in which God calls people to special service. We have by-passed calls of the prophets Jeremiah (Jeremiah 1:4-10) and Ezekiel (Ezekiel 1-3), and the disciples (Matthew 4:18-22; 9:9; John 1:35-51). We have also omitted further consideration of the heroes God called in the book of Judges, such as Gideon (6:1-24), Deborah, and Barak (4:4-10). The reader will undoubtedly think of other call narratives that could have been, and perhaps should have been included here. But having pointed out the trail, I leave further exploration to your discretion. Here, it is time to look back over the terrain we have covered and ask what have we discovered; did we find what we expected or did we manage to escape the trap of seeing only what we were look-ing for? What have we learned from these stories about when God calls? I think four themes have emerged that merit a final glance.

God's Call and Me

The "Me" generation may have been replaced by Generation X, the MTV Generation, the Boomerang Generation, Generation Y, and the Internet Generation, but we have not been superseded. Our cul-ture still revolves around the individual—me, my desires, my inter-ests, my comfort, and most of all, my happiness. And unfortunately, this is not just a "secular" value; it resides deeply within many churches where community has been replaced by a collection of spiritually self-seeking individuals. Commitment to the larger group, the church, the community, or even the world, extends only so far as it benefits my personal relationship to God.

> **God's call is bigger than my self-restricted world, and when God calls it is not about resolving my own personal issues.**

For this reason, the first theme that has surfaced from our study must be cast in the negative: God's call is not about me, never has been and never will be. Moses, as we have seen, had a hard time with this concept. He thought God's call relied on his status, his abilities, and most of all, his desires—what he wanted or did not want to do. Moses learned that God's call was not about any of that, not about him at all. We have seen others also strug-gle with this lesson. Jonah had a selfish streak as wide as a Category 5 hurricane. He wanted no part in any call that did not suit his purpos-es, but only tasks that revolved around Jonah's security and happiness. And Jacob was willing to take his place in God's plan only when God came through with a shopping list of blessings just for Jacob.

God's call is bigger than my self-restricted world, and when God calls it is not about resolving my own personal issues. If anything,

God's call creates rather than resolves individual spiritual crises. Just ask Moses, Isaiah, Abraham, Sarah, or Mary; life was calmer, more settled, much easier before God called than after. But God called them anyway, away from themselves and their narrow interests to bigger concerns—God's concerns for their society or world. And that just created problems for the one called. Israel is enslaved, oppressed in Egypt; Moses is free and living happily miles away. Judah is in serious trouble with God and ignorant of just how deep they have dug their grave; Isaiah is a devoted follower of the Lord in Jerusalem. The world is dying for a Messiah whom they will kill once He arrives; Mary is just a kid in Nazareth. Not one of these people needed or wanted a special call from God to complete or fulfill their own spiritual lives. God's call, instead, just caused them trouble.

That's the way God's call works in all of the texts we have studied. God calls people to become part of His plan for resolving issues bigger than me. And as a resultant corollary to this point, God's call is often not what I would expect or prefer to do with my life. Given a choice, the people called by God in the Bible would rather decline—and would back out of God's call if it was just about them, but it's not.

Seeking God's Call

I have been surprised by when God's call comes in our stories. To be sure, most who are called were already devout followers of the Lord, although not all (e.g., Jacob). Most also seem pre-disposed or open to the will of God in their life, even if they may be confused at the moment (e.g., Saul). But unless I have missed something, not one of our case studies involves a person looking for a call from God. Those God called were not anticipating a call, much less looking for God to speak to them.

There was a common practice in the ancient Near East in which a person, typically a king, prophet, or priest would "incubate" themselves in a holy place (e.g., a temple) to solicit a dream/word from God. And we may see a few scattered instances of such incubation in the Old Testament. Solomon seeks a word from the Lord by offering sacrifices and, apparently, staying at the tabernacle in Gibeon, and as a result God responds in a dream (II Chronicles 1:1-13; I Kings 3:4-15). Saul also attempts to gain direction from the Lord through a dream, but reports the failure of this medium as well as prophets and the Urim (casting lots; I Samuel 28:6). There is, however, no indication that anyone in our texts had incubated themselves to solicit God's call. Jacob's call is similar to incubation, but he does not realize he is on a holy site, nor is he seeking a word from God. I suppose it is possible that Samuel had incubated himself to seek a word from God; he was in the sanctuary at the time of his call. But Samuel is not waiting for God's call to be a prophet; when it comes he is confused and surprised.

The theme that has come into view is that God's people did not receive a calling by sitting around waiting to hear the voice of God or trying to discern the will of God for their lives. It might be nice if that's what happened in these stories and thus, what we should do. But it didn't and we shouldn't. Instead, those God called were living out faithful lives when God interrupted. They were in the middle of doing what God had already placed before them to do: Moses was raising sheep and a family; Joshua was serving Moses and Israel; Samuel was working in the tabernacle; Zechariah was at work in the temple; Mary was growing up faithful to the Lord. God's call comes when it is least expected to people who are already doing what they understand to be God's will (even Saul), not when a person is waiting and watching for a sign from heaven before they do anything.

These first two themes sometimes work together in vicious cycles: When I forget that God's call is about God and not me, I tend to obsess with discerning God's call for *my* life. And I discover, all too often, that what I am doing is searching or hoping for a call that

I prefer over what is already before me, something more glamorous, something with more prestige, or as Paul might put it: I want to be a hand, not a toenail in the body. Meanwhile, I stop doing what God has put before me until I "discern" God's call for my life. It's somewhat of a Jonah move, just not as dramatic as hopping a ship to Tarsus.

God's Call—Direct and Indirect

God has a flair for dramatic calls: visions of a quaking, smoke-filled temple, angels climbing up and down on a ladder extended between heaven and earth, blinding lights, and burning bushes. More often, however, the spectacular is by-passed (or not recorded) in favor of the simple: "The word of the Lord came to Jonah" (Jonah 1:1), "the Lord said to Abram" (Genesis 12:1), "the Lord spoke to Joshua" (Joshua 1:1), or "the Lord called, 'Samuel! Samuel!'" (I Samuel 3:4). In these cases God's call came in the form of an audible voice, perhaps a voice that originated from the ark of the covenant where the Lord sat invisibly enthroned on the Cherubim (Samuel) or from the sky and only the one called could understand it (Saul). God's voice might also come from a prophet who delivers God's summons (e.g., Elijah calls Elisha, I Kings 19:19-21) or an angelic messenger in human form (Genesis 18:1-15). Or the source of the voice may remain unidentified (e.g., Genesis 12:1).

The evidence does suggest, however, that when the Lord "spoke" or the word of the Lord "came" to call a servant it was audible, not an inner impression or feeling. Words to denote impressions or feelings are available in the Hebrew and Greek language, but these are not the words we find in God's calls. I'm not saying that God could not call a person via internal modem, some direct stream of ideas that summons a person to service or that God may speak to them in this way after their initial calling. But this is not what God did to call people in the biblical call narratives. We just don't find anyone reporting a direct call from God by saying "God laid it on my heart" or "I feel that God has called me." I don't doubt that God can call people in this way or however God pleases. But we should at least acknowledge that much of the language associated with Christian calling today is not biblical, not what we have found in our study of the texts. And this discovery should cause us to be more cautious with our vocabulary and claims.

> **If we are anxious to receive God's call...we should not stop our ministries to wait for a direct word or vision from God.**

Aside from the direct, spectacular, visionary, voice of God callings in the biblical text, the more common form of calling comes indirectly, through the community of faith. In the Old Testament the needs of the community were often met by the community discerning, selecting, and authorizing servant leaders (e.g., Bezalel and Oholiab [Exodus 31:1-6]), just as the early church called and commissioned elders, deacons, and apostles ("sent-out" evangelists). Pound for pound, people called through an intermediary far outnumber those called by direct means of visions or voices, at least according to the record we have in Scripture.

Again, these first three themes combine into a greater whole. If we are anxious to receive God's call, a call that centers outside of my self-interests in God's kingdom plans, we should not stop our ministries to wait for a direct word or vision from God. Quite the opposite, we should engage ourselves into the work of God before us; it is the faithful servant who is given more talent, more responsibility, not the servant who refuses to put his one talent to work (Matthew 25:14-30). We do need times of solitude, times of spiritual reflection, and should seek these out. But these spiritual disciplines were never designed to solicit direct calls from God, but to work with the spiritual direction available through the community of faith.

Trust the God Who Calls

In our study of Abraham and Sarah, I claimed that the first task for those called by God is to trust the God who calls them. And despite by-passing this theme in other chapters, it is a major issue of every call narrative. Moses must trust the God who calls him to supply the words, power, and success or he will fail. Joshua must trust the Lord to split the river and collapse the walls. Jacob needs to believe that this God is trustworthy, worthy of him making the Lord his God. Isaiah has to believe that the Lord knows what he is doing in calling him to a ministry of failure. Saul has to change the object of his trust. Mary and Samuel will have to rely on the Lord in ways they never imagined. And Gabriel censures Zechariah for his failure to believe. In many respects, God's call to all of these was a call to faith, trust–their specific tasks were almost secondary.

The writer of Hebrews begins his catalogue of heroes with the definition: "faith is the assurance of things hoped for, the conviction of things not seen" (Hebrews 11:1). He spends the rest of the chapter explaining how it was by such faith that Noah, Abraham, Moses, Gideon, Samuel, and others called by God responded and endured by faith. Certainly, God's call set these people apart, but the writer's primary argument is that what made them heroes was their faith, not their call. They had a faith by which they embraced God's call, stepped out to do the unthinkable, and endured to the end. These heroes do not form a special club of elites because they were called by God. Rather, the writer reminds his readers that we are all "holy partners in a heavenly calling" (Hebrews 3:1; see also 9:15), that God has called us just as He called them. Thus, our aim should not be receiving a call equal to theirs; we have already received an even greater calling (Hebrews 1:1-4; 2:1-4; 3:1-6; 9:11-14; 12:18-24). What we need is faith to embrace God's call and endure.

No doubt we could identify other major themes that emerge from these texts and our study, but these four seem to stand apart. God's call is not about my selfish interests or even my personal spiritual fulfillment, but about God's hopes for this world. Most often those whom God calls are faithful servants already engaged in God's work and the majority of these do not receive direct, spectacular, miraculous calls, but indirect calls through the community of faith. And the chief task for every person who ever received a divine call is to trust the God who calls and step out in faith.

The God Who Calls

From the beginning, God has chosen to work through people to accomplish His goals for the world. It's a risky move, relying on weak, fickle humans who may balk at God's attempts to use them, get confused about their role, make a mess of the task, or do what God asks them to do with less than god-like attitudes. But that's our God—a risk taker who believes in us much more than we believe in Him. God places His faith in Abraham and Sarah to leave home and follow Him; He relies on Moses to go back to Egypt. God looks to Isaiah, Saul, and Samuel to take His word to the people. Perhaps there was a Plan B or maybe some of these calls were already Plan B, but that's beside the point. Whether Plan A, B, C, or D—God's consistent plan is to entrust His work to people.

God does not, however, leave us alone. In his first letter to Thessalonica, Paul put it this way: "The one who calls you is faithful, and he will do this" (5:24). In the context of this statement, the "this" that God will be faithful to do is sanctifying us completely and keeping our "spirit and soul and body" sound and blameless at the coming of the Lord (5:23). The point here, and we have seen this throughout our study, is that what God calls His people to do, God empowers His people to do. God does not call a servant to a task, wish them the best of luck, and then leave them to their own devices. In almost every instance, this is the newly called servant's worst fear and the basis of their objections: we cannot do this, the obstacles are too great, we are not capable.

God's call on our lives, direct or indirect, entrusts us with awesome responsibility. Who are we to be conduits of God's blessing to the world? By what right do we speak words from God to our world? How can we ever accomplish what God has called us to do? And God's response is as uniform today as it was in every story we have read: I will be with you. I am calling you, placing my plan in your hands, trusting you with my work. But I will never leave you. Even in the Lord's final words to His apostles, when He called them to go out and make disciples of all the nations, He made this emphatic: "I am with you always, to the end of the age" (Matthew 28:20). God calls us, commissions us to His work in the world, but we are never alone; Immanuel, God is with us.

Discussion Questions:

1. In your study of "When God Calls," what has been the most important or helpful lesson you have learned? Why? Other than the major themes mentioned in this chapter, what themes have emerged in your own study?

2. If you could add one more unit to this study, what would it be? Why? In what ways might you or your group tackle this omitted subject?

3. What do you understand God's call to be on your life today? How have you arrived at this understanding? Did you ever expect God to place this calling or task before you? Why or why not?

4. Reflect on prior calls of God on your life. To what has God called you in the past? How did you feel about these tasks or roles? Did you feel adequate or inadequate? In what ways did God supply your needs to accomplish the call?

5. Allow time for your discussion group to describe what they see as each person's gift or calling from God. Remain silent as the group discusses your call. Then, after the group has completed discussion of each member, have each member share their responses to the group's observations. Does the group's assessment agree with your own? What surprised you? Why?

6. The opening chapter described two different attitudes toward calling in the Stone-Campbell movement, one rooted in our past suspicion of special calls from God and the other in recent concerns to discover our calling. Where did you place yourself on this spectrum of attitudes when you began this study? Where do you place yourself now? In what ways, if any, have your attitudes changed?